PRAISE FOR *DO IT! SELLING*

"*Do It! Selling* is overflowing with practical, actionable guidance that works in the real world. David's ideas will change your entire relationship with revenue. It's worth 1000x whatever you pay for it."

Jay Baer, co-author of *Talk Triggers: The Complete Guide to Creating Customers with Word of Mouth*

"Sales can be and should be fun. And if anyone can help you with that, it's David Newman. David gives you one actionable idea after another (77 of them to be exact). *Do It! Selling* is not only a fun book, it's also an important book. Implement what David teaches, and you will see tangible results—even if you think you don't like sales!"

Bill Cates, CSP, CPAE, author of *Beyond Referrals* and *Radical Relevance*

"*Do It! Selling* has taken all the guesswork out of sales. David gives you the step-by-step HOW of effective selling, which is so crazy important. This is my new go-to reference to get ahead with better clients, to stay ahead by closing bigger deals, and to move ahead faster by knowing what I'm worth. Win-Win-Win."

Judy Hoberman, president, Selling In A Skirt

"Whether you're leading a professional services firm of one or one thousand, the key to boosting your income is to get better at sales. You can't rely on referrals. You can't count on word of mouth. You must DO IT, and lucky for you, *Do It! Selling* is the missing instruction manual you've been looking for."

Laurie Guest, CSP, CPAE, author of *The 10¢ Decision*

"If you're a professional services seller and you want to sell deals bigger, better, and faster than ever before, *Do It! Selling* is for you. David's rapid-fire 'do-this-now' style will give you the mindset, toolset, and skill set to raise your game and fill your bank account. You'll start selling more even before you're done reading."

Lee B. Salz, author of *Sales Differentiation* and *Sell Different!*

"At its core, it is never a sales issue, it is always a trust issue. Even before that, the best professional services sellers trust themselves. That is where David Newman's *Do It! Selling* will help you the most, because David gives you the frameworks and principles to help you sell from a place of authenticity, curiosity, and service."

David Horsager, author of *The Trust Edge* and *Trusted Leader*

"Just being a 'people person' isn't enough to master sales. *Do It! Selling* is your go-to-market playbook if you're responsible for business development and you want real results. David gives you fast, actionable changes you can make in your sales attitude, sales behavior, and sales conversations that pay off big. When you're ready—and you are—let David be your guide to selling smarter."

Brynne Tillman, CEO, Social Sales Link

"Selling. Better. Now. That's the essence of *Do It! Selling* in three words. David gives you the paint-by-numbers system to grow your leads, clients, and revenue. If you're a driven entrepreneur and you want to sell more B2B services, grab this guidebook for growth and follow David's wise advice right to the bank."

Suzanne Evans, *New York Times* bestselling author and founder, Driven Inc.

"I have strongly advised David Newman against publishing *Do It! Selling* because this content should only be revealed in a $10,000 sales workshop, NOT in a $30 sales book. It's simply too valuable, and David is defrauding himself of hundreds of thousands of dollars by sharing such clear, simple, and highly effective strategies for not only how to land bigger deals but more of them. Assuming David ignores my advice, and you happen to find a copy of *Do It! Selling*, you'll save $9,970 when you buy it, devour it, and most importantly pick one idea, use it for profit ,and then dive back in for another. And another. And another. You'll be hard pressed to run this well of wisdom dry."

Tom Poland, multi-time bestselling marketing author

"*Do It! Selling* is a great book, and combined with David's other book *Do It! Marketing*, it amplifies your skills in marketing and sales 100 fold. You'll get enormous value from this book. Actionable, no-nonsense sales strategies and tactics are on every page. David intimately understands the mindset and sales challenges of consultants, because as you read his books, you start to feel that you can really do this. If you want to overcome your marketing and sales reluctance, and get results fast, this book should be your bible, sitting on your desk at all times with concepts highlighted and pages earmarked."

Taz Sadhukhan, co-founder, Centricity

"Don't buy this book. It will only bring you more business than you can handle in your professional services firm. And then you'll need to hire more people, expand your thought leadership platform, serve way more clients, and make a lot more money. Nobody wants that. Seriously—just don't. Stay small. Stay scared. You're not ready for *Do It! Selling*. Or are you?"

Ellen Melko Moore, founder, Supertight Social Selling

"If you're building a business around your expertise, *Do It! Selling* takes the mystery and anxiety out of sales and shows you how to create a selling system that perfectly matches who you are. Once you do that, your sales success is inevitable."

John Jantsch, author of *Duct Tape Marketing* and *The Ultimate Marketing Engine*

"Unlike so many sales books, *Do It! Selling* is written specifically for trusted advisors who love their work but don't love the sales part. David Newman will change all that in this fast-moving book filled with smart ideas to help you sell with relevance, relationship, and value."

Rod Santomassimo, author of *Knowing Isn't Doing* and president, The Massimo Group

"David's book is much more than a practical sales handbook for professional experts. *Do It! Selling* will help you completely reconstruct your 'Selling DNA' from the ground up. Highly recommended."

Danny Iny, CEO of Mirasee, author of *Teach Your Gift* and *Effortless*

"Man, oh man, I wish I had David's book 15 years ago when I started my consultant journey. Coming from a corporate sales job, I knew how to sell but I didn't know how to sell myself, and I didn't know how to apply those sales lessons to a solo practice. If you are a consultant, coach, speaker or thought leader, this is the only way that you should be selling. I loved it!"

Chris Baylis, founder, The Sponsorship Collective

"Boom!!! That's the sound of your professional services firm exploding with the growth ideas inside *Do It! Selling*. Part field guide and part sales rocket fuel, David has written the must-read, must-do book for every professional expert."

David Priemer, author of *Sell the Way You Buy*

"If you're an agency owner or consultant, *Do It! Selling* contains exactly everything you need to unlock your sales potential. Selling is an art form that is equal parts self-esteem, expertise, process, structure, leadership, relevance, and relationship. David hits on all these drivers with actionable simplicity. If you are looking to close premium clients, you must read this book right now. If you are like me, you will highlight, write in the margins, and dog-ear almost every page."

Robert Patin, author of *The Agency Blueprint* and CEO, Creative Agency Success

"As both a digital marketing agency owner and professional speaker, I can tell you that what David Newman teaches in this book WORKS. *Do It! Selling* helps you sell authentically by keeping sales simple and human. David shows you how conversation leads to conversion. If you hate selling, you'll start to like it. And if you love selling, your sales are about skyrocket!"

Corey Perlman, author of *Authentically Social* and *Social Media Overload*

"So many truth bombs on every page. It is EASY to start an expert business. It is HARD to sell effectively and consistently. Do yourself a huge (and profitable) favor and make sales exponentially easier with *Do It! Selling*. Buy this book now. Read it now. DO what David says."

Commander Mary Kelly, US Navy (ret), author of *Who Comes Next?: Leadership Succession Planning Made Easy*

"*Do It! Selling* is jam-packed with sales insights and highly action-able tips—bam, bam, bam, one right after another. As a resource that professional services sellers will keep dipping back into, it's awesome because it touches on such a wide variety of topics. It's a wealth of sales knowledge that you'll want to keep by your side to sharpen up your sales game."

David Jenyns, author of *Systemology* and founder of SystemHub.com

"If you want to sell with influence—and you do—*Do It! Selling* is your blueprint for success. David shows you a sales process that enhances your status as a thought leader, and one that you will enjoy using. Perfect if you are in the business of expertise."

Stacey Hanke, author of *Influence Redefined*

"David Newman isn't your typical sales expert. *Do It! Selling* isn't your typical sales book. David has no patience for sales BS, and he expects you don't either. What David delivers is clear, actionable, and proven ways to sell your expertise. No holds barred and no punches pulled, this book is filled with straight-to-the-point sales insights guaranteed to help you get more clients NOW."

Bruce Turkel, author of *All About Them* and *Is That All There Is?*

"I've led a 20,000-person consulting practice and I've been a solo consultant and speaker for over 20 years. David Newman gives you the no-nonsense, in-your-face perspective on becoming massively successful in professional services sales. No matter what size your firm is, *Do It! Selling* is truly the shortcut to your next level of growth."

Stephen Shapiro, author of *Invisible Solutions*® and *Best Practices Are Stupid*

"If you're a badass at what you do—consultant, branding agency, business coach, or service provider—it's about time you became a badass at sales, too. Lucky for you, David Newman shows you how to take your selling skills from 0-100 miles per hour in his usual no-BS style. *Do It! Selling* gives you absolutely everything you need in one tactical, practical, and totally DOABLE package."

Pia Silva, author of *Badass Your Brand* and founder, No BS Agencies

"If you're serious about closing more and better high-fee clients, *Do It! Selling* is your roadmap. David fills every page with exactly-how-to tactics to boost your sales. There is no better book to get you fired up, give you clear and concise action steps, and prepare you to sell more right NOW. Read this book—re-read it—and reference it often!"

Amy Yamada, producer of the VIP Day System TM and founder, AmyYamada.com

"In his signature no-bs, no-fluff, 'here's exactly what to do and say' style, David Newman has provided a masterclass—actually, no...a PhD—in how to sell. *Do It! Selling* is a concise, immensely entertaining book that doesn't waste a word. Regardless of whether you are a grey-bearded sales veteran producing at the highest levels, or an introverted solopreneur who would rather have your fingernails removed with a flame than talk to a prospect, you will find step-by-step methodologies and word-for-word frameworks you will feel completely comfortable using. And the best part is that all of this stuff WORKS. No gimmicks or cringeworthy, sales mumbo jumbo. David gives you solid, tested-in-the-trenches ideas, processes, methods, and messaging that gets results. Everyone sells every day. Get this book and you'll do it better."

Art Sobczak, author of *Smart Calling: Eliminate the Fear, Failure, and Rejection from Cold Calling*

"My own journey as a solo consultant taught me the truth of what David Newman says near the beginning of his masterful book, *Do It! Selling*: 'Sales success is (slightly) harder than it looks, but much easier than you've been making it!' Sales is not getting someone to buy something they don't want, but rather, sales is leadership. Following David's advice, as soon as you realize that it isn't your job to convince anyone of anything, the pressure falls off your shoulders and you're free to lead. To lead, all you need is self-confidence and conversational skills. *Do It! Selling* will give you a major upgrade in both."

Dov Gordon, CEO of Profitable Relationships and founder, Joint Venture Mastermind Group (JVMM)

"I'm all about the ABCs—Always Be Closing! However, you can't close if you don't have the right systems in place. *Do It! Selling* gives you absolutely everything you need to sell bigger, bolder, better, and faster to get results you've only dreamed of before. Go BIG! Do it NOW!"

Jeffrey Hayzlett, primetime TV and podcast host, speaker, author, and part-time cowboy

"Ahhh, finally! *Do It! Selling* unboxes, unpacks, and unravels everything you need to know about how YOU can sell better and sell more. You're getting a massive collection of easily digestible sales tools, tips, and ideas—all of which are sprinkled with David's signature humour and charm."

Geoff Ramm, author of *Celebrity Service Superstars* and global keynote speaker

"There are two types of professional service providers. Those who don't like selling and those who don't sell. The good news is David Newman's book, *Do It! Selling* is here to help. This is a must-read for every professional expert. What happens next is up to you."

Phil M. Jones, author of *Exactly What to Say* and creator of How to Persuade and Get Paid

"If you're just starting out, *Do It! Selling* is your 'Easy Pass' to get your revenue up and running fast. If you've had some success but are still struggling with getting and closing clients, this book has your missing pieces with kick-butt mojo to make sales easier (and more fun!). And, if your sales are strong, but you're wondering who to trust to boost them even higher, David Newman will reveal the subtle, significant shifts you need to make to rocket your revenue to the next level. Until I met David and used his advice, generating revenue was hard and selling was my least favorite activity. Now it's how I operate...because his approach works again and again and again!"

Mary Foley, founder of REV UP Society for Women Entrepreneurs and host of the *Live Like Your Nail Color* podcast

"Intelligent prospecting and human-to-human selling isn't new. But you've never seen it all laid out from 'high-level' to 'eye-level' the way David Newman does in *Do It! Selling*. It's like having a smart, funny, insightful sales mentor at your side for every sales conversation from initial contact to signed contract."

Sam Richter, creator of the Sales Intel Engine and CEO of SBR Worldwide/Know More

"This is the perfect sales book for business coaches. David is a genius when it comes to outlining a sales process custom designed for trusted advisors—especially those who feel uncomfortable with selling as a whole, and with sales conversations in particular. In *Do It! Selling*, David so appropriately calls out the 'Vortex of Crazy' around all the things everyone is telling you that you should do in selling, and then brings the conversation back to easy-to-grasp big picture ideas, smart sequenced strategies and frameworks, and clever in-the-moment tips that will allow you to sell in the exact right way for YOU and who you are. The concepts he shares will make selling easier, more comfortable, and more effective, whether you're new to the business or an elite veteran."

Simon Bowen, founder of The Models Method

"I read every page of *Do It! Selling*. Every. Single. Page. You should too. Here's why, and what separates *Do It! Selling* from the zillion other sales books on the market: David Newman gives you implementable advice that will absolutely work for your solo consulting firm. It's not dense, technical or theoretical. Nor is it rah-rah fluff; every page is packed with value. This is the real-deal sales book you've been looking for, and seriously action-oriented. *Do It! Selling* is packed with specific, detailed frameworks, scripts, examples, direction, suggestions and exercises that will move you and your business forward. Read it today. (You'll thank me tomorrow.)"

David A. Fields, author of *The Irresistible Consultant's Guide to Winning Clients* and founder, Ascendant Consulting

DO IT!
SELLING

www.amplifypublishinggroup.com

Do It! Selling: 77 Instant-Action Ideas to Land Better Clients,
Bigger Deals, and Higher Fees

For more information, please contact:
Amplify Publishing, an imprint of Amplify Publishing Group
620 Herndon Parkway, Suite 320
Herndon, VA 20170
info@amplifypublishing.com

Library of Congress Control Number: 2022919827

CPSIA Code: PRV1222A

ISBN-13: 978-1-63755-563-7

Printed in the United States

DAVID NEWMAN, CSP

Author of *Do It! Marketing*®

DO IT!
SELLING

77 INSTANT-ACTION
IDEAS TO LAND
BETTER CLIENTS,
BIGGER DEALS,
AND **HIGHER** FEES

an Imprint of Amplify Publishing Group

CONTENTS

PART 14
ENGAGE!

PART 15
THE CLIENTS YOU DON'T WANT

PART 16
F.U.

PART 17
THE PSYCHOLOGY OF HIGH FEES

P

Prologue

PROLOGUE

NO

There, we got that out of the way.

Everything you're expecting from another same-o, lame-o sales book you can throw out the window right now.

No tired cliches.

No empty promises.

No "sales 101" basic blocking and tackling.

There are over 70,000 sales books currently in print, so trust me: you can find all that crap elsewhere in abundance.

Unlike those 70,000 sales books, I wrote this book for a very special person:

YOU

- The solo expert
- The consultant
- The executive coach
- The corporate trainer
- The professional speaker
- The online course creator
- The mastermind facilitator
- The trusted advisor
- The sage
- **The thought-leading professional services seller**

You're a smart expert with something to say and something to sell.

If that's NOT you, then you have 2 choices:

1. Put this book down right now (oh, wait, there are still physical books?!)
2. Read on and see what professional services sellers need to know and DO, whether you're a company of one or one thousand

Your first step in moving from **information** (this book) to **implementation** (your results) is to grab all the free training, templates, resources, and companion tools waiting for you at **www.doitmarketing.com/selling**

DON'T

If you're still here, then chances are good that you...

- Don't have a sales manager
- Don't have a sales territory
- Don't have sales quotas
- Don't have a sales department
- Don't have sales meetings

And most importantly, as you decide if the "juice is worth the squeeze" for you to keep reading this book right now...

You.
Don't.
Like.
Sales.

SALES CAN FEEL LIKE A MYSTERY

It sure did to me back when I started my business in 2002.

Perhaps you feel the same way.

And perhaps you have the same beliefs I did, such as:

- "I'd rather get a root canal than spend another minute selling, pitching, and peddling my stuff"
- "Cold calling and being a desperate spammer? No thanks!"
- "Old school high-pressure sales tactics don't work for me"
- "Sales seem so random to me. Sometimes it just happens, sometimes it doesn't"
- "There must be a more systematic way to market and sell"

Back when I left my corporate job and started out as a solo consultant and trainer, I thought my #1 job was consulting and training (Yay!)

Turns out, I was wrong: my #1 job was SELLING that consulting and training (Boo!!)

I was terrible at prospecting.

I couldn't close a door, much less a sale.

I didn't seek help, because I thought I could figure it out on my own (Wrong!)

This caused me to waste 3+ years in needless struggle and financial instability.

Sales success is not a mystery.

It's just a series of simple decisions, and the action steps to implement those decisions, that will help you regain the **clarity, confidence, and control** you need to reach higher levels of success.

LOUD AND PROUD

Let's get this out of the way right now:

You ARE a salesperson.

As soon as you embrace that fact, your sales results will start to improve.

It's your role, it's your job, and it is the sole source of your professional money-making capability.

Wear that label proudly and make it part of your identity.

The longer you reject it, deny it, and avoid it...

The less money you'll make, the less impact you'll have, and the less value you'll deliver.

Listen, I agree with you...

Yes, you ARE a professional services expert.

Yes, you ARE the founder and CEO of your company.

Yes, you ARE a trusted advisor and mentor and coach.

AND...

Yes, you ARE a salesperson.

Throughout the rest of this book, when I use the words **salesperson** or **salespeople**, I am talking about YOU.

SALES IS (NOT) HARD

Let's face it: it's easy to get discouraged in sales.

Rejection is part of the game.

But I have great news:

Sales success is (slightly) harder than it looks, but it's a heck of a lot easier than YOU'VE been making it!

Too many professional services sellers overcomplicate, overthink, overanalyze, and overparalyze themselves before they even start.

Where does that come from? It comes from fear, hesitation, doubt, and a whole bunch of negative self-talk around sales and selling.

Where does the negative self-talk come from? It comes from your past experiences with bad sales training, bad sales process, or bad sales prospects.

Time to let all that go.

Nice deep breath please...there it is. Good job!

Don't be too quick to throw in the towel because you lost a sale or two, because you hit a brick wall, or because you let an opportunity slip through your fingers due to lack of persistence.

Otherwise, the negative momentum starts to build, you start EXPECTING rejection, you start PERCEIVING rejection that isn't even there.

Soon you're not answering your emails and voicemails ("Why bother? They're not going to hire me anyway."), you stop engaging on social media, and you're letting thousands of dollars disappear into your self-induced fog of discouragement.

Because you're reading this book, we're not going to let that happen to you.

In the upcoming 77 chapters, you'll find everything you need to achieve lasting sales success, even if selling has been the bane of your existence for your entire professional career.

Get ready to embrace your role as salesperson-in-chief of your business.

THE VORTEX OF CRAZY

When it comes to sales and selling strategies, it's no wonder you might feel dazed and confused.

You're caught up in the vortex of conflicting sales advice.

When you tune into webinars, go to conferences, watch YouTube videos, read sales books, or even just check your email inbox, you'll immediately see what I'm talking about.

YOU HAVE TO BE ON TWITTER! Social selling, baby! No tweets = no sales!

WAIT, SALES IS ALL ABOUT COLD CALLING! 100 cold calls a day, yep, that's the ticket. That's how I built my business and that's how you will build yours. And here's all the cold calling scripts you need for the low, low price of just 97 bucks!

WHAT? YOU'RE NOT USING SPEAKING TO GENERATE LEADS? Everyone knows that speaking is the best lead generator of all. Speaking to a group is like having 50 prospect conversations at once. You're deathly afraid of speaking? C'mon, join Toastmasters or hire a coach. If you're not speaking at events, you're missing out on a ton of sales!

NO, HANG ON. SALES COME FROM NETWORKING. Networking is sales and sales is networking. Your network is your net worth. The Chamber! The ladies auxiliary! The library basement circuit. The business card exchanges. Join my networking group! That is where to meet people and get referrals and introductions. Shaking hands and kissing babies. Even a small child knows this. C'mon, it's networking time!

LIVESTREAMING IS WHERE IT'S AT! *Flip on your camera and let's make some videos. Facebook Live, LinkedIn Live, YouTube Live. Salespeople now have a virtual TV studio in your pocket and [gasp!] you're not using it? Holy smokes, it's the only way to reach serious prospects. Video killed the radio star, so get those green screens fired up and go live, go live, go live!*

ACTUALLY, I FORGOT. IT'S WEBINARS! THAT'S YOUR SALES ENGINE. *Teaching sells. Grab your PowerPoint, and let's put some juicy testimonials and case studies in there. Oh, and don't forget you have to tease, plant seeds, give them the "what" but not the "how," build in urgency, scarcity, bonuses, and use all those tricks you learned from the webinar gurus. Master the webinar game, and the sales will pour in!*

Confused yet?

I sure am!

Here's the truth:

There is no ONE way to sell.
There is only YOUR way.

And it has nothing to do with tools, tricks, or technology.

So please stop trying to do every tactic under the sun.

Stop the sales monkey work and focus on direct-to-prospect activity.

If you listen to all the crazy, conflicting advice hurled your way daily, you will be forever distracted, confused, and overwhelmed.

It's time to stop the crazy and start the money.

Most salespeople actively want to improve their skills and increase their sales, but they keep using the same old formulaic sales approaches over and over again with limited results.

This book will give you renewed hope and, more importantly, new sales principles, sales strategies, and sales tools for selling smarter.

Many sales books concentrate on prescriptive tactics and manipulative tricks. This approach suggests that in sales, "one size fits all."

The truth is that **one size fits one**, and the key to unlocking your sales performance is experimentation and personalization in order to systematize your own brand of sales success.

You can't learn what you need to be successful in sales from just parroting phrases or using gimmicks you read in a typical sales book.

There is no cookie cutter. You're no cookie!

In this book, you're getting a powerful combination of sales methodology, practices, and principles that can immediately be **adapted, flexed, and integrated** into your daily selling activities to produce tangible results.

You'll be relieved and excited to learn you don't have to use canned methods or stilted scripts.

You're going to use your own personality, strengths, and preferences to zero in on EXACTLY what works for you.

This "real time, real world" approach is the key to sales success. Why?

Because you're not following MY system. Instead...

You will create your OWN system that uniquely fits YOU and your prospects.

You're getting the A-to-Z toolbox of proven principles of exactly what works to connect with buyers today, from first contact all the way to signed contract.

BORING DOESN'T SELL

Boring ideas die.

Boring salespeople lose.

In short, you want to be the opposite of boring.

You want to stand out from the crowd.

Where can you zig where everyone else zags?

Where can you break the sales mold? Or create a new mold that you (and you alone) are perfectly designed to fit by tapping into buyer psychology so that you quickly gain deep insights into exactly what your prospects, want, need, and value?

PANDEMIC TERRORIST MELTDOWN WAR

Name any crisis, whether it's 9/11, the financial meltdown of 2008, the pandemic of 2020, the Ukraine war of 2022.

At any of those times, there were salespeople who thrived and salespeople who got whacked hard.

Listen, you need to recession-proof your sales skills for the long term.

There WILL be more disruption, terrorism, or some other tragedy that will sideline average sellers for months, if not years.

It's not a question of "if" but a question of "when."

Applying the mindset, skillset, and toolset in *Do It! Selling* will ensure YOU are never sidelined again.

By applying the ideas in this book, you can sell successfully even in times of turbulence, transition, and turmoil.

WHAT YOU REALLY, REALLY WANT

You want to sell smarter to today's buyers who value empathy, relevance, and intimacy over sales pitches, sales hype, and sales nonsense.

You want to not only bolster your bank account, but you also want to become a better entrepreneur of your expertise.

Meaning you want to sell more, more easily, and more often.

Sales will feel better, smoother, more organic, and more conversational.

Your prospects will feel less pressure and become more open, more honest, and more communicative because of the human-to-human sales strategies you'll start to use.

If you're like most of the smart experts I work with daily:

- You feel that "old school" tactics (cold calling, ads, and spam) are useless and "there MUST be a better way"
- You're already working hard, but there's too much to do, never enough time, and sometimes you're not even sure where to begin when it comes to getting in front of the right prospects...
- You want to earn attention from prospects by positioning yourself as an authority with magnetic sales strategies that pull (not push) buyers to you...
- You want to sell more without chasing, begging, or scheming
- You want to make more money from prospects eager and willing to buy
- You want to waste less sales time, sales effort, and sales energy
- You want the sales process to be more effective, honest, open, and fun

- You want to focus on helping before pitching and serving before selling
- You want to land better clients, bigger deals, and higher fees
- You want to get out of your sales rut and find your sales groove
- You want to make selling a natural extension of who you are

If you are ready to kick your sales results into high gear, you're in the right place.

Strap in, hang on, and let's DO IT!

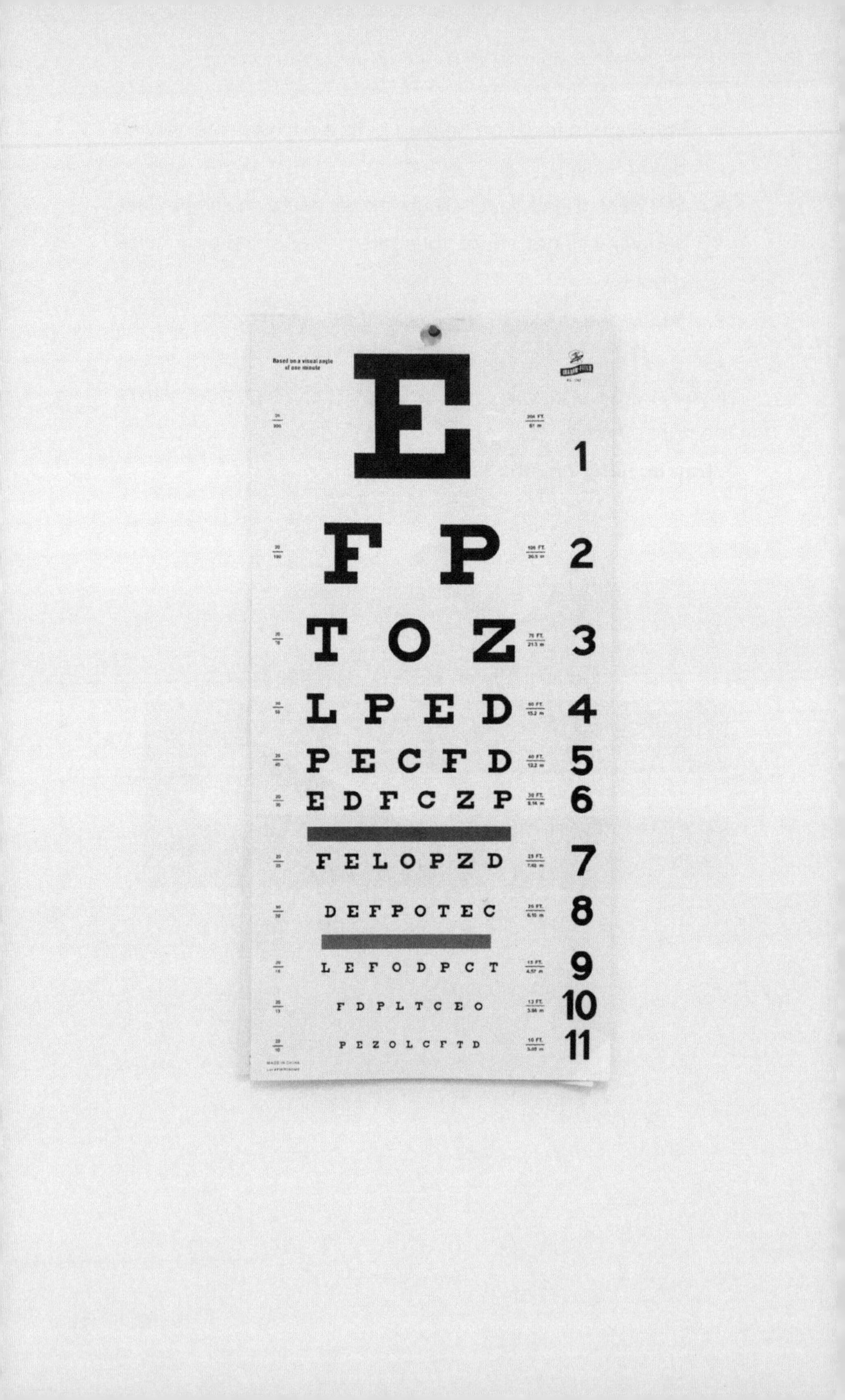

Based on a visual angle of one minute
E 1
F P 2
T O Z 3
L P E D 4
P E C F D 5
E D F C Z P 6
F E L O P Z D 7
D E F P O T E C 8
L E F O D P C T 9
F D P L T C E O 10
P E Z O L C F T D 11

1

Self Check

1 SELF-WORTH & SELF-ESTEEM

These are probably the two biggest obstacles to your sales success.

Self-esteem is how you view yourself in terms of yourself.

When you're alone, singing in the shower, you are a total rock star:

"Wowza, you are a great singer! And look at yourself in that steamed-up mirror. Sure, you're 20 pounds heavier than you like, but you still got the moves, Hot Stuff!"

Self-worth is how you view yourself in terms of others:

"Uh-oh. Is that broccoli in my teeth? I should have worn that other blouse. I hope they don't ask me if I've worked in their industry before. I should've updated my website before this meeting. What if they ask if I have a PhD? I'm afraid they won't take me seriously."

Most of us are fine when it comes to self-esteem, but self-worth is where things tend to break down.

Here are some pointers about self-worth that will help you improve your sales results:

Be a better person. One of my early sales mentors once said, "David, you know, you're so concerned about being a better salesperson. Don't worry about being a better salesperson. *Be a better person, and more sales will happen.*" This is about listening more carefully, caring more deeply, and being more open, empathetic, and curious. All of which we'll talk about in the pages ahead.

Don't worry about not being *good* enough or *smart* enough. People don't buy from you because of your credentials or because you have fancy letters after your name. They buy from you because of

- Your certainty that you can help them
- Your certainty about your expertise
- Your certainty of your relevance, value, and results

Help more people, connect with more people, have more conversations, add more value to the people that you would like to recruit as your next client.

Focus on outcomes. People never buy your products and services and programs. What they really buy is positive outcomes. In your sales conversations, everything needs to be about their team, their company, their problems, their challenges, their goals, their results, and arriving at the ultimate destination that your clients want to get to.

Remind yourself of your own awesomeness. At some point along the way, you may have simply forgotten how awesome you are, and you need a reminder. This is it.

Keep a "success" file. To remember your client success stories, keep a file of all the thank-you emails, letters, cards, and notes that you've received. I have an electronic folder and a paper folder in my filing cabinet labeled "Kudos." Kudos is slang for congratulations. When I'm having a bad day, when I'm not looking forward to my next sales call, when I'm a little bit down on myself, I will open that kudos file. And then very quickly after flipping through it, I am reenergized and recharged.

Always be ready to blow your own horn and lead your own parade. Because if you're down on yourself, if you don't think you're the greatest thing since sliced bread, why in the world would your prospects think so?

2 REMINDER: YOU=FABU!

You are now going to get in touch with your own fabulousness.

Grab your favorite pen and a pad or journal.

Write down your **5 favorite testimonials** from all sources: your LinkedIn recommendations, client evaluation forms, thank-you cards, emails you've received, social media posts about how you "totally blew the doors off" or provided "amazing value" or helped someone transform their business or their life.

Now let's zoom out and ask yourself the following questions, writing down your answers as you go.

Don't think. Just write down instinctively the first thoughts that come to your mind.

You don't even have to use complete sentences; short phrases and key words are fine.

Think bullets, not paragraphs:

- **What do you receive compliments about?**
- **What do people ask you to do?**
- **What do people seek your advice about?**
- **What consistent themes and patterns do you notice from your responses above?**

You will use these insights as the rocket fuel for your *Do It! Selling* journey, and they will help you redefine your sales activities and sales strategies.

3 YOUR BIGGEST FANS

You're going to have a little one-on-one contact with your favorite clients, champions, and raving fans, otherwise known as the people who know you and love you.

This is best done with your past and current clients, but even if they've never given you money, they should have experienced you and your work.

Let these fans know that you're sharpening your sales language and would love their help.

Then ask them for a quick 15-minute phone or Zoom call.

You will want to record this call because they're going to say some amazing things about you that you'll want to capture verbatim.

Ask these questions:

1. Why did you come to us/me in the first place?
2. What problems were you looking to solve?
3. Why do we/I still have your business?
4. How have we/I made your life and business better?
5. What results do you expect to create because of our work?
6. What results have you already gotten?
7. How do you feel now compared to when we first started working together?

To download this exercise in electronic form and grab all your free *Do It! Selling* templates, tools, and training videos, go to **www.doitmarketing.com/selling**

2

Sales Brain Upgrade

4 DO YOU LOVE SELLING?

Not only do you need to believe in yourself, but you also need to believe in selling.

This is the world of high fee sales. Done the *Do It! Selling* way, your sales process itself will bring value, insights, and new ideas to your prospects.

Succeeding in this world is going to depend on your *mindset*.

Because even the world's best sales strategies, tactics, tools, and scripts won't help you if you don't have the right mindset.

Let's do a quick quiz:

Do you love sales?

or

Do you dread sales?

Do you continually practice and sharpen your sales skills?

or

Do you let your sales skills get rusty, creaky, and stale?

To sell differently, you must feel differently.

For any sales task, from prospecting to discovery to following up to negotiating fees to closing, or even when you go to schedule sales tasks in your calendar, you might feel:

Anxious. *This initial call is going to be a disaster. I always get tongue-tied, and it gets awkward and weird.*

Depressed. *Oh God, not more prospecting. Can't I just focus on client work?*

Paralyzed. *Where do I start? I don't even know what a good sales process looks like. I'm already stuck.*

Overwhelmed. *This is too much work. I don't have the time. Fuggedaboutit!*

Mystified. *I was never good at selling anything. I don't have the sales gene. How am I supposed to sell myself and my services?*

Do you look forward to sales and do you block time for it daily? Probably not.

If you're like most of my clients, you find every possible excuse under the sun *not* to make time for sales.

Lead generation, prospect research, sales outreach?

You would much rather do a hundred different things, right?

You'd much rather create a new slide deck for your upcoming presentation.

You'd much rather write an article.

You'd much rather shoot a video.

You'd much rather work on your next book. (Sort of like what I'm doing as I write this!)

Because you love the creative work.

You love the client work.

You love seeing the light bulbs over your clients' heads when you're training or coaching or doing a virtual speaking engagement.

Harsh Truth: You can be the world's greatest coach, consultant, speaker, or expert, but if you don't have paying clients, you don't have a business.

No sales = No clients = No money = No bueno.

You're not going to get the income and the joy and the meaning you want from your business UNLESS you master your selling skills in a different way; one that is organic, a way that you find easy, effortless, enjoyable, and even (dare I say it?) fun!

5 INVITATION TO CONVERSATION

To think of selling in a new way, let's start by redefining the word.

Selling is an "invitation" process.

It's an invitation to a conversation.

Who's afraid of an **invitation**?

Well, typically nobody; invitations are usually good.

What happens when you get an invitation?

You go to a party with either cake or bourbon or barbecue. All good so far, am I right?

Who's afraid of a **conversation**?

Usually, we look forward to conversations. They're engaging. You learn things and you get to meet cool people and exchange ideas with them. Some of those people may even become your new best friends.

If you reframe your sales thinking, you will look forward to those sales invitations and sales conversations in the same way.

Maybe even more so, because not only are you conversing with your new best friends, but you're also conversing with your **new next clients.**

With every new prospect conversation, imagine you're recruiting to fill a job position, and the job title is "My Next Client."

If you are interviewing people for that job, you have nothing to fear, nothing to hide, and you have all the power.

Why? Because YOU are conducting the job interview!

You're evaluating them (even more than they are evaluating you) to make sure that they're a great fit and that they're the exact kind of client with whom you can do your best work.

In my previous book, *Do It! Marketing*, I suggested you redefine *marketing* in four words:

Offer value. Invite engagement.

Now I invite you (see what I did right there?) to redefine *selling* in four words:

Send invitations. Spark conversations.

6 WHAT IS A SALES PROCESS?

Let's start to demystify this concept of a sales process.

A sales process is the series of consistent steps you take every prospect through from initial contact to signed contract.

Depending on what you're selling, a sales process might take anywhere from a single phone call or Zoom meeting to several weeks or months.

Ultimately, your job is to make your sales process and its corresponding phases as short as possible.

As a consultant, trainer, speaker, coach, or expert, your sales process will be relatively short.

You'll use 5, 6, or 7 steps because this is not a complex multi-zillion dollar industrial sale. You're not building oil rigs in the Persian Gulf.

Your sales process becomes your playbook and your safety net to make sure that every sale rolls out the way that you want it to.

A sales process is simply a set of repeatable steps that you follow to convert prospects into clients.

Let's pretend these are stages in your CRM (Customer Relationship Management) software or columns in a simple spreadsheet:

Step 1. IDEA: The moment you identify a potential prospect for your services, you put that prospect in the Idea column.

Step 2. CONTACT MADE: When you do your first outreach, whether that's a phone call, email, LinkedIn connection, whatever it might be, you move that prospect to "Contact Made."

Step 3. CALL SCHEDULED: When you've booked an initial Zoom meeting or exploratory call, they move to column three.

STEP 4. CONVERSATION: Once you've had your initial conversation with them, they move to column four.

STEP 5. SECOND CONVERSATION: Once you have a follow-up conversation with them, they move to the Second Conversation column.

STEP 6. EMAIL FOLLOW-UP: Once you've emailed some additional details, they go to column six.

STEP 7. DECISION CALL: And once they're ready to make a yes or no decision, meaning you're closing the deal or booking the final meeting, it's a decision call and they move to column seven.

This is all driven by follow-ups in **their** calendar. You don't leave it open. You don't just say, "Sure, I'll call you next week."

Never leave one step of your sales process without a commitment from them for a next step, with a hard date and time written into THEIR calendar.

To download a companion resource on this topic and grab ALL your free *Do It! Selling* templates, tools, and training videos, go to: **www.doitmarketing.com/selling**

3

Audition Your Prospects

7 YOU SET THE STAGE

As an entrepreneur, you set your own rules.

And your rules are based on the kind of business you *want* to create and the kind of revenue you *want* to generate.

You have the power to decide:

- **Who are your target clients?**
- **What kind of work do you want?**
- **What kind of fee level do you want for that work?**

Those are the decisions you need to make if you want to consistently generate better clients, bigger deals, and higher fees.

It's not about wishing or hoping to be successful; it's not about accepting whatever clients or projects fall in your lap.

It's about setting up guardrails and standards in your business so that sales happen daily, and you always know where your next client is coming from.

8 IT ALL STARTS WITH WHO

To audition actors for a movie, you must know the character you're casting.

You must decide what you want them to look like physically. Are they tall, short, thin, fat, a sweet-faced ingenue, or a big bad villain dude?

You need a clear idea of what range they can play emotionally, physically, and intellectually. Are you casting for a truck driver or a ballet dancer?

Taking this back to your business and client selection, here are three questions for you:

1. Who's your ideal client?
2. Who do you really want to connect with?
3. Who would you love to have a door-opening conversation with?

If you say "everyone," "anyone," or "whoever wants what I sell..."

Those are all bad answers because you're very likely to cast the truck driver in the role of the ballet dancer (Nobody ends up happy seeing that movie!)

The two most powerful words in sales are:

DECIDE

and

DEFINE

Decide who to target.

Define exactly where to find them.

The salespeople who struggle with this are the ones who are looking for "signs from the universe," or who are waiting for a definitive pattern to emerge from their past sales successes.

You're making this harder than it needs to be.

There is no "big reveal." If you're waiting for the sales gods to part the clouds of confusion as the rays of sunshine beam down on you, and you're waiting to hear them sing in angelic harmony, "You should sell to engineering firms," well, that's not going to happen.

Ask yourself these questions:

1. Who do you get the best results for?
2. Who did you really enjoy working with at any phase or stage of your career?
3. Who would be fun to work with? What kind of company and what kind of client do you really admire?
4. What kind of engagement would be exciting and challenging?
5. Who are some of the big dogs in your industry who would give you instant credibility and that marquee name recognition?

Then look at it from the negative perspective:

What are the knockout factors that tell you, "This client isn't for me?"

1. Is the company way too big?
2. Way too small?
3. No money?
4. No problem?

5. No urgency?

Don't make this decision overly complex.
Stop chasing squirrels.
Stop hedging your bets.
Decide and define!
Remember this key *Do It! Selling* mantra:

Target what you want. You can always take what comes.

In other words, your proactive outbound prospecting should be **highly focused, targeted, and specific.**

If a prospect outside your niche or target market approaches you, of course you can take that call and bring on that client IF you want to.

I will never tell you to turn away business, "No, I'm sorry. You're IBM; I only work with banks. Please shred that $50,000 check you were about to give me."

But those are the exceptions.

You can't target 12 industries at once. That only causes frustration, overwhelm, and burnout. Sound familiar?

Cool. Then STOP it!

4

The Likely Suspects

9 THE BEST OF THE BEST

Finding the right people to talk to can make or break your prospecting success.

Here are some quick ways to identify prospects you want to reach out to.

1. Use the media.

Look at your local business journal, the business section of your local metro paper, industry news, trade and professional publications, the Book of Lists that might be in your metropolitan area, and see **who's being interviewed, profiled, and promoted.**

2. Aim high.

Aim high in a large organization. And **aim for the top** if it's a small to midsize company.

In a large corporation, you have **hundreds** of buyers, not just a few!

If you're going after that big multinational corporation, look at the VP level, senior VP level, executive VP level, VP of sales, VP of marketing, and so on. Look for senior leaders by division, geography, business unit, or brand.

For example, a quick LinkedIn search I just did while writing this chapter generated 696 executives with the title "Vice President" at healthcare giant Johnson & Johnson.

If you're selling to small and midsize companies, it's easier to reach out to the top. There's one president, founder, or CEO.

There's one VP of marketing, one VP of sales, one VP of HR. Get their contact info, plan your approach, and you're good to go!

3. Target the best.

Every year there are hundreds of lists of the best companies in different cities, industries, and for different aspects of work life.

Use these lists to identify the individuals who are seen as "the best" and who are making things happen.

Here's the guiding principle behind this strategy:

The best of the best are the ones who invest.

Yes, that rhymes.

And yes, please staple that concept to your forehead. Or make a sign with big letters and hang it on your office wall (less painful).

Why?

Because you don't want to do a lot of convincing, persuading, or cajoling in your sales process.

The best way to avoid that is to connect with prospects who "already get it" and don't need a lot of convincing that what you're trying to help them with is important and valuable.

You also don't want to go after laggards who are in terrible shape. Ironically, it's these prospects who need you the most but will never buy.

Let me repeat that because it's so vitally important if you want to stop wasting a ton of time looking for love in all the wrong places:

The prospects who need you the most will NEVER buy.

Stop looking for prospects who NEED you. Start connecting with great prospects who WANT you so that they can get ahead, stay ahead, and move ahead faster.

If you are US-based and you're looking for leaders inside companies who value their culture, their people, and employee satisfaction, then start with lists like *Fortune* magazine's "100 Best Places to Work in America."

But don't stop there. You can also look for "best places to work" and "best employer" lists at the **international level and the state level** (50 US states = 50 lists!) and even in major cities. Best companies to work for in Seattle, Chicago, Philadelphia, Rome, Paris, Berlin, Rio de Janeiro, Tokyo, Sydney, and so on.

If you're working with executive women, you'll find lists such as "Fortune Best Workplaces for Women," "Forbes Best Employers for Women," "Best Companies for Women to Advance," "101 Best Global Companies for Women in Leadership," and many more.

If you're working in the diversity, equity, and inclusion space, you'll find lists such as *Black Enterprise*'s "50 Best Companies for Diversity," DiversityInc's "Top 50 Companies for Diversity," "Best Employers for Latinos," "Top Companies for Asian American Executives," "Best Companies for Multicultural Women," and "Best Places to Work for LGBTQ Equality."

If you're working with young professionals, you'll want to check out the Career-Launching Companies list, Best Companies for Career Growth, Fortune Best Workplaces for Millennials, Best Companies for Young Professionals, Canada's Top Employers for Young People, and many more.

If you help companies with health- and wellness-related issues, you'll find lists such as "40 Best Corporate Wellness Companies," "Healthiest 100 Workplaces in America," and again, at the regional level, you'll find lots of "healthiest companies" and "best companies for wellness" in various states and cities.

Are you looking for high-achieving executives and entrepreneurs? Check out local and regional lists of "30 under 30" and "40 under 40." These can also be industry specific, such as "40 Under 40 Emerging Community Bank Leaders," "40 Under 40 Champions of Construction," and "40 Under 40 Top Diverse Talent in Silicon Valley."

One set of awards overlooked by many people, but shouldn't be, are awards celebrating the best in a certain profession or job title.

Take a minute right now and check out all these juicy search engine queries:

- CEO of the Year Awards
- CFO of the Year Awards
- CIO of the Year Awards
- CMO of the Year Awards
- HR Executive of the Year
- Financial Executive of the Year
- Sales Executive of the Year

There are lists upon lists upon lists that will help you discover the best of the best.

Want all these juicy leads delivered straight to your inbox in real time? All you need to do is set Google alerts for all the relevant search terms above.

Let me repeat that: **juicy leads delivered straight to your inbox.**

For laser-targeted prospecting, it doesn't get much better than that!

10 17 REASONS TO SELL TO THE TOP

What's the difference between a professional practice (or company or expert) that feeds on the bottom versus YOUR business, which should aim to **serve the top of your market?**

Here are 17 things to consider:

1. High fees are paid by clients and customers who are **doing well**, not those who are struggling.

2. Referrals come from those who are **proud of the fees** they pay you, not ashamed to be lowballing their way through business.

3. High-end clients tend to be **believers**; low-end clients tend to be skeptics.

4. Top clients are **easier to please** because they have a partner attitude, whereas low-end clients are almost impossible to please because they have a peddler attitude.

5. **Paying higher fees also means** your top-of-market clients pay you higher respect, pay your advice more attention, and invest more resources in their implementation of your ideas.

6. **There is always a way to raise your game**, boost your value prop, and charge higher fees; otherwise, we wouldn't have $500,000 sports cars or $35,000 watches.

7. **There's no profit** in a business model that challenges other poverty-mindset entrepreneurs in a race to the bottom.

8. **You can always design a "lower-level entry point"** to a high-end offering (example: the $195 Tiffany bracelet); however, it is almost impossible to "level up" from commodity

status. In other words, Walmart would have a tough time attracting high-end jewelry buyers.

9. **Are you attracting referrals to goofballs** or people who don't see the value of what you offer? Like attracts like. It's very possible your current clients and customers simply don't travel in the right circles.

10. **If you've heard yourself say**, "My clients won't pay any more than they're already paying," or "I can't raise my prices, because I'll price myself out of the market," then you may need a.) better clients, b.) a new market, or c.) both!

11. **High-end clients expect great work**. It is energizing, engaging, and fun for you and your team to rise to that challenge.

12. **Low-end clients expect perfect work**, even though they have no idea what they want, change what they want based on whims, and are a moving target of conflicted priorities. It is demoralizing, exhausting, and depressing for you and your team to put up with these micromanaging, neurotic control freaks.

13. **High-end clients value relationships,** and once they're in with you, they'll come back for more. Why? Because if they switch, they would essentially be admitting to themselves that they overpaid or made a wrong decision, which is more expensive to their ego than to their pocketbook. Bottom line: high-end clients always look for reasons to stay.

14. **Low-end clients only care about transactions**. The next coupon or email or offer will lure them away for the next bargain. They're forever playing *Let's Make a Deal*, and the fact that they bought from you once REDUCES the

chance they'll buy from you again. Bottom line: low-end clients always look for reasons to leave.

15. **High-end clients will approach you with new ideas**, ask for more innovative services, and help you develop new products and programs that they WANT to buy and that people at their same level would value. They serve as your personal idea-generating R&D department to help you grow your business.

16. **Low-end clients will pressure you to give less**, offer "lite" versions, and generally dumb down and dilute your core offerings to match their small thinking and tiny budgets. Don't fall for it.

17. **Companies that serve low-end clients are** dependent on massive numbers of small transactions from one-time buyers and price shoppers. **Companies that serve high-end clients** thrive on small numbers of much larger, deeper, richer, and longer-lasting relationships with clients, customers, and friends who stay longer, buy more, come back more often, and refer like crazy.

It's your call: serve the top or serve the bottom.

Just be careful what you wish for, and know what you're in for when you get it!

5

Get After It!

11 THERE IS NO BLUE

Where did that lead come from?

"It came out of the blue."

How did that client find you?

"They found us out of the blue."

What made them call?

"They called out of the blue."

How many times have you heard yourself give these types of answers?

Hmmmm…me too.

Until one night when I was having dinner with The Hot One™ a.k.a. my lovely bride of 38 years.

I was telling her about a new client, and she asked me, "How did they find you?"

I instinctively answered, "I dunno. They found me out of the blue."

By the way, this is a terrible answer for a sales guy to give.

Back to dinner with The Hot One™. She looks over at me, pauses meaningfully, and says…

"There is no blue."

Ouch. And she's right. She made me think harder, look harder, and connect the dots to find out where and how this client came to me. I should've known exactly how my specific sales activities attracted this specific client.

This is a terrific reminder for YOU too…

There is no blue.

Here are 14 potential sources of inbound leads who become prospects.

You need to work harder at identifying, specifying, and inquiring about these when GOOD prospects come your way.

And even more so when, like in my situation, good prospects become clients!

1. Google (or other search engines)
2. Your articles in hard-copy publications (industry magazines, trade journals, association publications)
3. Your articles posted online (guest blogs, contributed columns, niche industry websites)
4. Your social media accounts (LinkedIn, Instagram, Facebook, Twitter, etc.)
5. Your blog, landing pages, and lead magnets
6. Your email campaigns and email newsletters
7. Paid advertising (online or offline)
8. Your personal network (friends, family, colleagues)
9. A referral (current client, past client, or nonclient fan or influencer)
10. Directories and listings (online, offline)
11. Your speaking engagements (local, regional, national, in person or virtual)
12. Your videos (on your website or sites like YouTube, Vimeo, etc.)
13. Your podcasts (the one you host or where you're the guest)
14. Your media interviews (TV, radio, online, print)

Become fanatical about tracing new leads back to specific sources.

Put a sign up on your office wall to remind you if necessary...

There is NO blue!

12 SMART VISIBILITY AND CREDIBILITY HACKS

You have a huge platform never before available to salespeople in the history of business.

Use it!

Before the internet, salespeople like you and me would have sold their children to get their hands on the research power, sales connectivity, and content creation tools that we enjoy and totally take for granted today.

It's time to get off the sofa, people! Make some noise, stir the pot, rock the boat, and let's get after it!

1. Write articles for industry publications.

Let's say your target market is financial advisors. A quick online search will show you that one of the big associations in that industry is NAIFA (National Association of Insurance and Financial Advisors). And a quick look at their website will tell you they have a national magazine called *Advisor Today*.

Reach out to the editorial staff and ask for contributor guidelines. In the case of the *Advisor Today* website, there's even a handy link on the main navigation labeled "Contribute." Everything you need is right there.

Once you start submitting value-rich articles to these editors, don't be surprised if one of the first questions they ask you is, "Do you have more of these? Would you like a regular column?"

Why? Because association magazines and industry publications are hungry for great content. In many cases, they need you more than you need them.

2. Launch a "Quoted and Featured in" strategy.

You want to build up your PR portfolio very quickly? You want to start getting featured and quoted in all kinds of industry and trade and professional publications?

Then check out PRLeads.com, a fantastic service run by my friend Dan Janal.

The PR Leads service sends you requests every day from reporters who are writing stories for major publications who desperately need to find experts to quote in their stories.

You get these requests delivered to your email inbox, along with the reporter's name and email address and their story angle so you can contact them.

All you do is you hit reply to the journalist, give them two or three sound bites for their exact request, add your brief bio, and if they like what you wrote, they'll either use it as is or call you for a brief interview.

If you have the information, insights, and opinions they need, they'll feature you and your business in their articles.

With PR Leads, there's no need for a $5,000 per month PR firm. Boom, you win!

3. Your own national newspaper and your own TV network.

With your blog or your LinkedIn account, you have the equivalent of a national newspaper at your disposal.

And you have a global TV network in your pocket called YouTube or LinkedIn Live or Facebook Live.

But are you using those just to post random content, or are you using those in the service of an intentional prospect-getting campaign every single week?

Do you have a content-rich blog that addresses your prospects' biggest pains, problems, heartaches, headaches, challenges, and gaps?

Are you posting something intriguing, challenging, or contrarian every week on LinkedIn?

Every day that you don't publish or post, that you don't put something in the marketplace that is designed to get the attention of your exact best-fit prospects, you're invisible.

Remember:

No one ever buys your expertise sight unseen.

If that's true, and it is, then your main job on a daily basis is to GET SEEN!

4. Everywhere you want to be.

WARNING: It is very easy to get scattered, distracted, and overwhelmed with social media monkey work.

That is the LAST thing I am recommending.

You want to have a focused, intentional, and highly targeted content strategy that pulls new leads into your world every day.

For example, I have been accused of "being everywhere" by some of my subscribers: "You're in my email. I'm always seeing your stuff on Facebook. I love your videos." And then the inevitable question: "How do you do it? You are EVERYWHERE!"

I'm not everywhere. I'm just everywhere my prospects are.

If you're running a delicatessen or a yarn store, you've never heard of me, and frankly I don't know why you're reading this book! Those folks will never see a single piece of my content. I will be completely invisible to them. It's like I live on a different planet.

But if you're a consultant, coach, speaker, trainer, or expert, you'll see me a LOT.

Because I know where you live.

And I know what you want.

And I work hard every day to give you everything you need so that you can get better clients, bigger deals, and higher fees.

The key to YOUR social media strategy is exactly the same.

The goal is to be like your VISA card:

For your prospects, show up "everywhere they want to be."

13 INTERVIEWS AS A PROSPECTING STRATEGY

How do you know what your prospects and buyers really want and need?

Not sure? Don't guess. Don't hope. Don't wing it!

Do some research. If you're evaluating several different potential niche markets or vertical industries, spend some time on researching each one.

Live in their world, think about their problems, and think about their clients and prospects. What's the first step? Data gathering. Preparation. Homework. Industry, regional, business, and company news is now at everyone's fingertips on the internet.

Look for articles, blogs, verbatim quotes from executives and industry analysts, video clips, podcast interviews, and capture as much as you can.

Then go directly to the source: real live customers and prospects.

Here is a simple, repeatable process for researching what types of services and programs your target market will pay for. You can use this strategy to improve your prospecting results immediately.

This is GOLD, and it's also one of the easiest and most enjoyable ways you can prospect, build relationships, and break down barriers to high-level decision-makers who might otherwise be unreachable.

Yes. It's. That. Good.

Forget that you're a consultant, coach, or expert.

As of right now, you're a writer, researcher, journalist.

Find the top trade association magazines or industry publications that your target executives read, recognize, and respect. And prepare to write an article for them.

Why? Because thought leaders do original research.

For prospecting purposes, this is priceless.

You access high-level buyers it would take you months to reach, if ever!

You establish yourself as an expert and a peer.

You have a good reason for a series of follow-up relationship-building opportunities.

First step: The title of your article series must contain an **embedded compliment.**

For example, "How Smart Leaders at Top Companies Profit from Breakthrough Innovations" (for an innovation consultant).

Or "How Top Producers at Leading Firms Create Referrals for Life" (for a sales trainer focused on financial services firms).

Ask 4–6 questions, such as:

- What's been the biggest factor in your success?
- What obstacles and challenges are you still working on?
- What's the best advice you've ever heard on this topic?
- In your opinion, what's the secret sauce that many miss?
- What's the key practice or tactic you keep coming back to?
- Crystal ball: What does YOUR next level of success look like in this arena?

Do these by phone or video, whichever they prefer (video is better for rapport).

Map out your approach and all follow-up touchpoints over the next 60 days:

Interview; thank-you email; thank-you card; send the finished piece; send a link to the interview on your blog; if local, offer to stop by and drop off a signed copy of your book; send a different article; invite them to a seminar; send a note ("another idea for you"); share a research report; send a video clip; plan to **send something every 7–10 days** that is of direct relevance to what they told you their top challenges and priorities are.

By the 5th or 6th week of doing this, you've earned the right to have a pivotal conversation:

"Hey, Bob, we've been talking a lot about solving your challenge with issue X. I think there may be some ways I can be more formally helpful to you. Would that be worth a short chat?"

Almost all your prospects will say yes, and a few will have asked YOU for help even before you send this request!

Do 3 of these per week = 12 per month. And in 60 days, you'll have 24 hot prospects (whom you hand selected), ALL of whom know your name, will gladly take your call, welcome you in their email inbox, and who probably look forward to hearing from you.

One client I worked with wanted to go deep into banks and credit unions. He used my interview strategy, and within a few short weeks he landed interviews with a dozen CEOs, including those of the 2nd- and 3rd-largest credit unions in the nation, plus the CEO of every major community bank in his home state.

From these interviews and following my advice, he landed a regular column in TWO national credit union industry publications.

He then sent me this email:

Very excited about the results:
- *Three paid speaking engagements at high-profile leadership conferences.*

- *A large systems project with a top-10 US bank.*
- *Launching a credit union CEO mastermind group.*
- *A yearlong CEO leadership intensive with the largest state-based CU trade association in the country.*

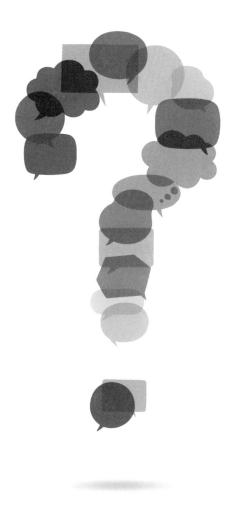

14 IF YOU WRITE THE TEST, YOU GET AN "A"

Another great way to dominate your marketplace as a consultant, coach, or professional services expert is to prepare a document that lists the 20 questions clients should ask before hiring someone like you.

If you're a leadership coach, yours will be "20 Questions to Ask Before Hiring Any Leadership Coach." If you're a social media consultant, "20 Questions to Ask Before Hiring Any Social Media Consultant." If you run a team-building company, "20 Questions to Ask Before Hiring Any Team-Building Company."

Here's the secret: If you write the test, you're going to get an A.

If you write the test so that YOU have all the right answers, then **you set the buying criteria** for your prospects.

This makes their decision easier, so you're truly helping them, and it makes YOU the standout obvious choice, so you're helping yourself at the same time.

Invest the time to write these 20 questions and send them to prospects early in your sales process. Because there's no better way to start a relationship than a conversation like this:

> YOU: *Are you looking at a couple of different consulting firms right now?*
> PROSPECT: *Yes, we are.*
> YOU: *Great. Let me send you a document that will help you make a good decision, whether it's with us or not.*

Here's a complete example based on our own Do It! MBA mentorship, which is designed for B2B consultants, executive coaches, speakers, and trainers:

20 Questions to Ask Before Enrolling
with ANY Business Coach/Mentor

1. Does the company specialize in working with solo consultants?
2. Is the mentoring format designed to suit varied learning styles?
3. Is there an exclusive focus on application and "do-this-now" steps?
4. Does the mentoring include built-in follow-up and accountability?
5. Does the mentoring tie into YOUR exact business issues?
6. Is there an online component to the program available 24/7?
7. Will I learn situational strategies in addition to personal skills?
8. Is the program relevant to ALL levels of consultants and coaches?
9. Is there a specialist team to help you, not just a single mentor?
10. Will I be intellectually stimulated enough to feel challenged?
11. How current is the content that I will be learning?
12. Will I get a complete library of templates, tools, and scripts?
13. Will I be learning from a proven, published 7-figure mentor?
14. Does the mentor have LOTS of verifiable client success stories?
15. Do I have access to an ongoing source of support between calls?

16. Will I get personalized feedback and "next best step" guidance?
17. Will there be NO hidden charges or fees once I enroll?
18. Does the mentor use and monetize the exact tactics they teach?
19. Is the mentor just a bored guru OR a full-time business coach?
20. Does the company qualify clients, or will they work with anyone?

When you send your own version of this to a decision-maker, it sparks a little bit of panic in their mind. They start to think, "Oh my gosh, I didn't ask that last consultant this question, and it seems kind of important." Who has the best answer right under the buyer's nose? YOU DO!

Because you wrote the questions to help them make their buying decision, you're automatically positioning yourself as the #1 choice. After that, any other experts they might consider are being vetted against YOUR criteria.

I'll stretch your thinking even further on this one: Your job is not to get hired. Your job is to help your buyer make the safest hiring decision that gives them the greatest feeling of confidence that they will get the results they want.

MAKE yourself the safest choice and watch how many new doors open for you when you knock!

To download this exercise in electronic form and grab all your free *Do It! Selling* templates, tools, and training videos, go to **www.doitmarketing.com/selling**

15 WARM AND FUZZY

If you're like most consultants, business coaches, and solo experts, your most underutilized prospecting asset is your warm network.

This is your circle of allies, friends, colleagues, and champions.

Look at the people you're already in communication with, whom you've already touched in some way, shape, or form.

Not sure where to begin building your list of your warm network?

Look at the last 30–40 people who you've

- Emailed
- Called
- Texted
- Messaged on Facebook, LinkedIn, Instagram, Twitter, etc.
- Zoomed with individually or in a group

Do you have an email newsletter that goes out via tools like Constant Contact, Mailchimp, HubSpot, etc.?

Look at the last 30–40 people who opened your email newsletter; then look at the last 30–40 people who clicked on one of your links in that email. Those are even warmer!

All kinds of people are going to start popping up. List them, and those people will make you think of other people who you're equally well connected with (or more so!)

Now let's cruise over to your social media platforms...

Look at the last 30–40 people who liked, commented, or shared one of your social posts.

Got a good list of people who know you, like you, and might even be looking for ways to help you?

Cool! Here's what to do with each of them:

Tell them exactly the kind of prospects you are looking for (be as narrow, specific, and clear as possible) and tell them 1-2 specific outcomes those prospects most want.

Example: "I'm looking to connect with 3 established solo attorneys who are ready to bring on partners and build a team so they can work less and get their life back."

Then ask:

"Do you know anyone who might be a good fit?"

You're not marketing to them directly, but you're unleashing some inbound referrals and some inbound introductions.

Your contacts are your ministry.

Don't let any of them go to waste.

What's the worst that can happen? Your request goes unanswered.

What's the best that can happen? Strategic introductions. Inbound sales conversations. And an army of fans who are now activated to help you find others who might be perfect clients for you.

That's how you unleash the magic of your warm network.

POP QUIZ

You are 5 sections into this book right now.

The title of this section is "Get After It!"

If you've gotten to this point, and you haven't already found several strong candidates to be your next client, then you are "just reading."

Remember the title of this book, *Do It! Selling*?

Stop "just reading" and start using these ideas to get into action.

Don't wait until you've finished reading the entire book before you start to get results.

I want this to be the most profitable **reading, deciding, doing, and selling experience** you've ever had with a book as your guide.

Hesitation is the enemy of sales success.

Just like with your prospects, "later" means "never."

As you read from now on, I urge you to follow this modified mantra from the United States Department of Homeland Security:

If You See Something, Sell Something.

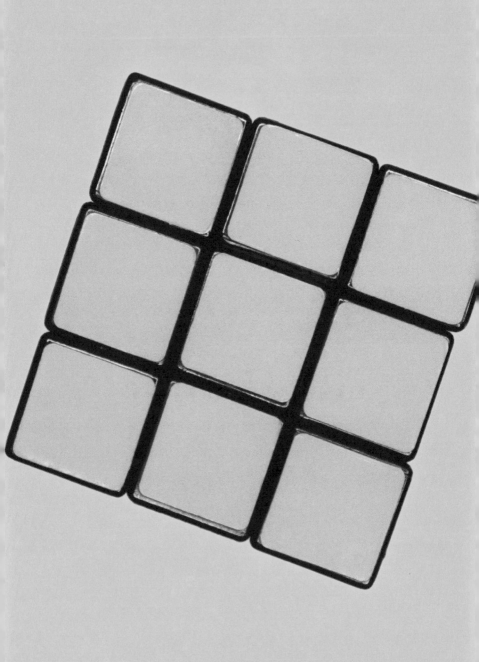

6

Now Get in The Game!

16 GET IN WITH BIG COMPANIES

At any given time, I recommend you have 20 active prospects in your pipeline: 20 specific human beings with whom you want to do business.

WARNING: By active prospects, I don't mean a broad idea of your "target market" nor a general description of your "avatar" (who sells to blue aliens anyway?) nor a detailed "buyer persona" named Wendy who is 35 years old, drives a BMW SUV, and has 2.3 kids.

I mean a written, finite, workable list of real prospects whom you want to do business with, whom you've researched, and whom you're ready to approach.

I call this list your **Active 20.**

For larger companies, develop an **Angles & Opportunities Profile,** which is a one-page research document where you can collect key information about their top executives, what they want, what they need, what they're working on, and what's strategically important to them.

It won't take long to put this together.

You'll find all the information you need on their website, on their media page, in their press releases, or in their annual report, plus any coverage from local, regional, national, or international business media.

Thanks to Google and LinkedIn, we're probably talking about **15 minutes of research.**

Take the information from your 15 minutes of research, using the Angles & Opportunities form available at **www.doitmarketing. com/selling**, then **connect the dots** to the value, impact, results, and outcomes YOU would bring to the table to help them solve those problems or accelerate those outcomes.

Now you're ready to make contact because now they have a reason to talk to you.

You're not going in blind. You've earned that first conversation. You know exactly what they're going through and exactly how your expertise, experience, and services fit into their landscape.

As a result, you're much more confident, motivated, and excited to talk to them and open a conversation about how you might be able to help them.

Here's what this looks like:

ANGLES & OPPORTUNITIES

Date: _____

Organization/division:

Contacts

Relevant C-suite executives:

Relevant VP level executives:

Source of information:

Opportunity

List out the problems, challenges, strategic initiatives, and breaking news in their world. Gather this from their annual report, press releases, media page, published interviews with key executives, media appearances, podcasts, videos, etc. Collect direct quotes and facts/statistics from these sources so you have them here at a glance.

Angle

Based on your research, what is the angle from which you can help them? What is relevant to your experience, expertise, and professional services that they could benefit from? Again, quote the exact words they've used on their website, awards they've won, strategic direction of the company, obstacles they would like to remove, and accomplishments they are aiming for.

Our value/services

Brainstorm some connections between what they NEED and what you DO. What are the areas of intersection, crossover, and overlap where you are a "perfect match" to help them get rid of a problem they have and do not want, or achieve an outcome they want but do not have? Show how you are the "bridge" that will get them from where they are to where they want to be.

Action taken

What did you do already? Did you connect on LinkedIn or ask your centers of influence for insights? Did you like, share, or comment on something they posted on social media?

Next step

❑ Research	❑ Network	❑ Write	❑ Email
❑ Call	❑ Package	❑ LinkedIn	❑ Send book

Outcome

❑ Phone mtg	❑ Meeting	❑ Referral	❑ Proposal

17 GET IN WITH SMALL COMPANIES

Let's move to prospecting strategies to get you in front of small and solo business owners.

If you're reaching out to individuals, you first need to get to know them as a group.

Where do they gather?

What do they read?

What online and offline groups do they belong to?

Good news: all this research is also at your fingertips, just like with the big companies!

Use Google to identify the associations, conferences, conventions, groups, and chapter-based organizations they belong to.

Read the magazines, newsletters, blogs, and association publications they read.

Find the online blogs, portals, communities, groups, and forums they hang out in and insert yourself into those conversations.

Start attending the online and offline local, regional, or national events they attend.

As my friend social media strategist and speaker Corey Perlman likes to say:

"Fish where the fish are, and you'll never go hungry again."

18 3 MISSING INGREDIENTS

If you're not selling what you want to sell at the fees you deserve, there are 3 missing ingredients to your "Now Get in the Game" prospecting plan:

1. **Lack of a clear, committed decision on whom you want as your clients.** Are you deliberately choosing the type of clients you want to work with? Or are you casting too wide a net and trying to be all things to all people?

2. **Lack of articulation and distinction** of how you talk about what you do and its value, impact, results, outcomes, plus the emotional payoffs of solving those problems or achieving those outcomes.

3. **Lack of daily proactive outbound sales activity** to a *finite*, *focused*, *written*, and *workable* target list of high-probability prospects.

How do we fix these three missing ingredients?

First, **channel your best clients**. Not your terrible clients, not your so-so clients, but your dream clients. Create three inventory lists: one for what they *want*, one for what they *need*, and one for what they *wish*.

Here's how.

Under a heading labeled "I Want," write down 10 phrases your best clients told you they want when they first started working with you.

Then do the same under the heading "I need" and again under the heading "I wish." Jot down 10 client "I need" phrases you hear a lot and 10 client "I wish" phrases you hear all the time.

There are two sources to help you create these lists quickly.

First, replay in your mind all the conversations you've had with buyers and with prospects.

Second, mine Google creatively. Let's say your clients are in the health-care field. You could do Google searches for:

- Biggest problems in health care today
- Top problems for health-care CEOs
- Health-care CEO survey
- Challenges for the health-care industry

Researching these issues will help you get to know your prospects intimately: what they want; what they need; what's missing, funky, broken, and sad in their world; what they'll value; and what they'll resonate with.

As a professional expert, you value **educated buyers** who know what they want and show up ready to invest with you.

Similarly, your prospects will value YOU much more highly the moment you become an **educated seller**.

19 GENERALIZE OR SPECIALIZE?

The #1 mistake you might be making as a professional services expert is this:

Positioning yourself as a GENERALIST.

I hear you, you don't even need to say it. Your biggest fear around specializing is that you will limit your options.

Right now, that's scary because you think you'll be "leaving a lot of money on the table" by narrowing your client base or limiting the type and scope of work you do.

That's what I thought too. And that's why the first three years of my consulting business were a total disaster.

Now here is the truth:

Specializing does NOT limit you. It FREES you.

It CREATES hugely profitable options.

You get to trade BROAD (commodity) for DEEP (highly specialized).

You will be able to work with dream clients whom you attract through your specialized marketing because you understand their specialized problems, desires, and challenges.

That means they feel especially understood. And they instantly see you as the specific expert they need to hire, not a commodity they can price shop.

You keep this specialized marketing machine running until you have more dream clients than you can handle.

Most generalist consultants and coaches must settle for whatever business falls in their lap.

And that's not a viable way to grow a sustainable expert business.

The other downside of being a generalist is that you're easily interchangeable with other generalists.

It is supereasy for your prospects to find a cheaper option when you're a commodity.

Experts win on value, and generalists die on price.

20 STOP DOING CRAP YOU HATE

To get in front of the right prospects, choose the method that suits your personality, your strengths, and your preferences.

If you love to **write**, use writing strategies. Create articles, blogs, cheat sheets, short guides, PDFs, worksheets, etc. If you hate writing, don't write. It's not going to work, because you're not going to keep up with something you hate to do. If you love **speaking**, use speaking strategies. Do virtual presentations, host webinars, use a podcast-guesting strategy, host your own podcast, or speak in front of targeted groups. If you love it, the more you speak, the more clients you'll get. If you hate it, then don't.

If you love **video**, use video strategies. Invest time and energy in building out a great YouTube channel. Go live regularly on LinkedIn and Facebook. Do a video blog. Use video email tools like BombBomb to get in front of prospects with your personality and charm. If flipping on your camera makes you break out in a cold sweat, then please don't even think about doing video. It's not for you.

If you love geeking out on **tech**, then use tech strategies. Love tinkering with search-engine optimization? Go for it, you SEO rock star! Want to futz around building a digital studio in your home office? Cool! Are you into using the latest AI tools for prospecting, content generation, CRM, and more? Are you loving some of the latest online collaboration tools, like mural.co, miro. com, and circle.so? Have at it, amigo!

Are you a **design** freak? Then design strategies are for you. Create your own memes, quotes, and wallpapers to share with your fans and followers. Create Canva templates and giveaways. Build out some cool designs and share them on your blog or email them to your list.

Do you love **networking**? Then use in-person and online networking strategies. If you love meeting new people, shaking hands and kissing babies, get out there and network your heart out. Mixers; online events; in-person meetings; regional or national conferences; local meetups; and connecting 1-on-1 at breakfasts, coffees, and lunches. They are all perfect for you if you love networking.

If any of the items above make you say, "I hate that crap," you now officially have my permission to STOP doing them immediately.

Focus only on lead-generating strategies you find easy, effortless, and enjoyable.

Because those are the only ones that will be effective!

21 DEATH TO MONKEYSPAM®

I've even put a little registered trademark symbol next to that term.

Now, we didn't really register that trademark.

So it's not quite legal (Shhhhh...) but I just love the term *MonkeySpam* so much because that's exactly how prospects see you when you're guilty of sending that generic one-size-fits-all message.

They think you're a **monkey**.

And they think you're a **spammer**.

This is bad.

And it's not how smart consultants, coaches, and trusted advisors do prospecting.

Let's talk about the real deal with prospecting.

Proactive prospecting needs to happen daily.

Continually refill your "Active 20" prospect list with targeted decision-makers and reach out for a **specific** reason with a **relevant** solution you believe could **truly** help them.

This belief is based on research, relevance, and fact-finding; not guessing, hoping, praying, or winging it.

Thus, this prospecting approach is not cold, not generic, and not MonkeySpam® because the world has enough bad salespeople and clueless consultants randomly spraying pitches at these poor prospects.

Your job is simple: do NOT become one of them!

Focus on serving before selling and helping before pitching.

So many otherwise capable salespeople and consultants send MonkeySpam®. It's generic, boilerplate, value-free nonsense.

Then they wonder, "Gee, why do prospects never return my calls? Why do prospects never respond to my emails? Why did I send 57 emails without a single reply?"

Bad news: All those MonkeySpam® messages and emails have gone into a marketing black hole because you've shown up on their radar like a sleazy peddler and not like a trusted partner.

Does doing better take some work?

Yes, it does, but you know what? It a lot less work than you think.

It's 15 to 20 minutes of research per prospect.

Do that and you will start to show up as a true trusted advisor and as a peer-level authority. Know what they're working on, what's important to them, what problems and opportunities are front and center for them right now in the moment. And connect everything you do, say, and ask with everything they want, need, and are focused on.

This one simple shift will help you become more **relevant, relatable, and valuable.**

22 LASER FOCUS ON MMA

My friend Scott Simons hammered this concept into my head over 20 years ago...

Business success is about one thing: MMA.

No, not mixed martial arts.

Money Making Activity.

Too many professional services sellers are NOT reaching their sales and income goals for one simple reason: they're not putting in the time on MMA.

How much of your time is engaged in actual *Money Making Activities*?

Probably a lot less than you think.

To begin, let's be clear about what a Money Making Activity is and what it is *not*.

- Wasting time on social media is not MMA
- Cleaning your office is not MMA
- 99 percent of the emails you read and write are not MMA

Well then, exactly what is Money Making Activity?

Money Making Activity is direct-to-prospect communication, meaning anything that moves a prospect one step closer to a contract, an agreement, a message saying, "Yes, let's do this. We're in. Where do I send the check?"

For example, reaching out to prospects on LinkedIn is MMA.

That doesn't mean just posting content on LinkedIn.

Writing a blog post or a LinkedIn article or a white paper is not MMA.

But if you have a piece of content you've already written, putting that content in front of a buyer in the service of a sales campaign is MMA.

When you send that content to an active prospect and write, "Hey, Jim, this article I just posted answers some of your questions from our last call. I think you'll find it useful. Feel free to share it with your team and let me know what you think," that is MMA.

Make a big sign and nail it to your office wall: "MMA."

Hold yourself accountable on an hourly basis to STOP wasting your precious selling time and refocus on MMA!

Throughout your day, stop to ask yourself, *Is what I'm doing right now a Money Making Activity? Or am I wasting time scrolling on Facebook? Am I rearranging my email folders? Is there some MMA task I could be doing instead?*

Some of our favorite clients make an MMA graphic and use it as their desktop wallpaper that's always visible on their computer.

One client even has a cool MMA image as her Zoom background. Nothing makes me happier than seeing her smiling face and the huge letters *MMA* behind her!

7

Reach Out and Touch Someone

23 5 PROSPECTING MISTAKES

I am not a big fan of flossing my teeth. I know I should. But I don't.

When my dentists asks, "David, how often do you floss?" my stock answer for years has been "Not as much as I should."

The real answer is ZERO, but the safe answer that prevents the "only floss the teeth you want to keep" lecture is the one I give.

Does this sound familiar when it comes to prospecting?

ME: *How much prospecting are you doing on a daily basis?*

YOU: *Not as much as I should.*

Let's unpack the 5 biggest prospecting mistakes that most professional service providers make.

1. Not enough prospecting activity, which includes zero prospecting activity!

Before you start complaining about not having prospects, ask yourself:

How much prospecting activity have I done in the last 24 hours? The last 7 days? The last 2 weeks?

You might be surprised at the answer.

The first prospecting mistake is simply not doing enough prospecting activity, and sometimes not doing any at all!

It's amazing, the results you do not get from the work you do not do.

2. "Spray and pray" prospecting.

Here's a real-life example of "spray and pray prospecting" and the results you can expect.

A newer consultant was complaining to me about the total lack of results she was getting with her prospecting up to that point. I asked her for more details on what she was doing, how she identified good prospects, and what she was sending them.

Turns out, she was simply "batch and blast" spamming her LinkedIn connections. She was hitting 50 LinkedIn contacts at a time with the same "copy and paste" LinkedIn message. Of course, that message was totally generic, totally impersonal, and totally ineffective.

She told me that she did this 12 times, hitting 50 different LinkedIn connections at a clip. Then with genuine surprise, she said, "I don't get it. I've reached out to 600 prospects, and I've gotten zero responses."

Yes. Exactly.

There is nothing that makes me madder than a lazy seller.

I feel like slapping them upside the head with the nearest phone book (kids, you can look that one up on Wikipedia. They're thick and heavy.)

Did she accomplish anything through this type of outreach?

You bet.

She just informed 600 decision-makers that she's a hopeless, hapless spammer and totally clueless when it comes to value-first outreach.

Call this approach what you want: "spray and pray" or "everyone's a prospect" or "spam the universe." No matter what the label, it never works.

3. No idea how to open the first 10 seconds.

The problem here is that you have no idea what to say or send in that first contact.

No idea what that first email should sound like.

No idea what the first 10 seconds of that LinkedIn voice message might sound like.

Result?

Outreach reluctance. Prospecting hesitation. No leads in the pipeline.

4. Not knowing which channel to use.

- Do I start with a voicemail?
- Do I send an email?
- Do I send a video email?
- Do I hit them on LinkedIn?

There are so many choices, so you end up doing nothing.

5. No clue what to say and send for that initial door-opening conversation.

You have no idea what approach to use to get the door open, or what to send to get the prospect to think, *Maybe this person is worth talking to.*

- Should you pitch?
- Should you send your 1-pager?
- Should you ask if they hire outside consultants?
- Should you send your program PDFs?
- Should you send them the link to your YouTube channel?

The answer to all of these is no, by the way.

Remember our mantra from earlier? Effective prospect outreach is all about 4 words:

Send invitations. Spark conversations.

24 4 PROSPECTING TRUTHS

1. It's not the quantity; it's the quality that counts.

Prospecting is not a numbers game.

It's a relationship game, and it's a relevance game.

No professional services seller needs to talk to 200 prospects a month. We're not selling commodity widgets here.

Talk to maybe 10 or 15 hand-selected prospects per month, which will get you three or four clients per month, at anywhere from $5,000 to $50,000 each.

For that math to work, you must laser focus on exactly the prospects you want.

2. Segment your prospects.

Segment your prospects into cold, warm, and hot.

Let's define those three stages very simply:

Cold: No relationship and no reason to contact them.

Warm: Existing relationship or good reason to contact them.

Hot: In conversation with you about solving a specific problem or achieving a specific outcome.

Trick-question alert: What do you do with cold leads?

Answer: nothing.

Real answer: you must warm them up before making contact.

How do you warm up a cold prospect?

Relevance and research.

Based on that research, you'll soon determine if that is a high-probability prospect for your services or not.

Two warnings to keep in mind:

Not every prospect is a good prospect.
Not every good prospect is a good prospect for YOU.

3. Qualify your leads.

Do your research.

Spend 15 minutes reading their profile and tracking their activity on LinkedIn. See if you can find them on Facebook or Twitter or Instagram.

Scan their company website for news, announcements, or their media page. If it's a public company, grab their annual report and pay special attention to the letter from the CEO.

Do a quick Google search on their industry trends, issues, and challenges, if you're unfamiliar with their world.

Scan industry news or the trade press in their field to see if any of their executives have been quoted or interviewed recently.

The better you are at client selection, the worse you can be at everything else.

The magic happens when you start talking to the right prospects at the right time for the right reasons using the right language.

4. Engage each prospect with 2–3 different communication modes.

When you do outreach, don't rely too heavily on any one mode of communication.

Some people are phone people, and they hate email.

Some people hate the phone and love email.

Other people are all about LinkedIn, and they are messaging their little hearts out.

The best way to reach out to a prospect also involves some common sense based on their industry or the type of work they're engaged in.

- Are they always on the road?
- Are they working from home?
- Are they usually on-site with their clients?

For example, if your prospect base is made up of doctors or teachers, good luck reaching them on the phone! They won't answer the phone when they're seeing patients or in the middle of teaching a class. Email is your best bet.

Prospects are going to be more reachable and more responsive in one communication vehicle rather than another.

There is no one "right" sequence.

Remember the good old days when sales trainers would say, "Here's how to prospect: it's call, mail, call."

Those days are over.

Don't email someone 17 times in a row.

Don't leave six voicemail messages in a row.

Mix it up with your modes of outreach: try email, phone, social media, private messaging. And the big hint is:

The mode in which they respond is probably the mode they prefer.

A multimode prospecting process will get you through.

To download a companion resource on this topic and grab ALL your free *Do It! Selling* templates, tools, and training videos, go to: **www.doitmarketing.com/selling**

25 VIOLENT PROSPECTING

General George S. Patton famously said:

"A good plan violently executed now is better than a perfect plan executed next week."

Do not wait.

Another key to the *Do It! Selling* philosophy:

Go before you're ready!

Let's get some sales conversations on the books.

Here's an easy step-by-step QuickStart prospecting strategy you can do right now.

Step 1: Send out an email or post on social media saying:

"I'm looking for 3 people who want [outcome] and [result] over the next [time frame]."

Example: "I'm looking for 3 consultants who want to double their monthly income and take their business online over the next 90 days."

Step 2: If it's a social media post, say:

"Comment below if you're interested, and I'll send you details."

If you emailed it out, say:

"Hit reply if you're interested, and I'll send you details."

These are called "hand raise" strategies, and they are the quickest way to surface some leads who are interested and whom you can start conversations with immediately.

Here's another strategy you can use right away: the "working together" email.

I'll share my example with you, then it's your turn...

The email looks like this:

> **Subject: Working together**
>
> *I'm looking for 3 solo consultants who want to add $20K per month to their revenue in the next 90 days.*
>
> *We'll look at your strategy.*
>
> *We'll look at your marketing, messaging, offers, and pricing.*
>
> *We'll find holes and opportunities and get you clients fast.*
>
> *Hit reply, and I'll send you the details.*
>
> *—David*

The email (or Facebook post or LinkedIn post, etc.) is step one.

Step two: they reply.

Step three: You respond with:

> **Subject: Re: Working together**
>
> *Thanks for your interest.*
>
> *Would you be open to answering a couple of quick questions to see if I can really help you or not?*
>
> *1. Briefly, what business are you in?*
>
> *2. What's your monthly revenue right now?*
>
> *3. What's your biggest obstacle to getting [outcome]?*
>
> *4. In 2–3 sentences, describe what you're working on right now to fix it.*

Keep these questions simple.

You might not need four questions. Use two questions, use three questions, whatever it is that you need to find out if they are a good fit.

When they respond to your questions the way you like, you have a real live prospect who is both interested and qualified.

Get them on a call and start closing some deals!

Why? Because you followed the mantra: **Go before you're ready!**

26 BE UN-IGNORABLE

If you want to get more traction with your prospecting, don't just reach out to one prospect at a given company.

Reach out to the top three, four, or five people simultaneously.

This makes you much harder to ignore.

You want to make yourself a subject of conversation.

Here's how it works.

You contact the CEO of a medium-sized company. We'll call her Rebecca.

At the same time, you contact Ellen, who is the COO, and Todd, who is the VP of sales.

When you write to Rebecca, you let her know that you've also contacted Ellen and Todd.

Likewise, when you write to Ellen and to Todd: each time, you let the person you're writing to know that you've contacted the other two.

Now the three of them are going to be on their internal email or Slack channel, and they will be talking about **you**.

> Rebecca: *Hey, did a guy named David Newman contact you?*
> Ellen: *Yeah, he did.*
> Todd: *Yep. Did he contact you too?*
> Rebecca: *Yes, I'm looking at his email right now.*
> Ellen: *Well, what do you think? Should we talk to him?*
> Rebecca: *We did just talk about our sales strategy and how we may need some fresh ideas. Who wants to handle this?*
> Ellen: *Todd, I think this is more in your wheelhouse.*
> Todd: *OK, I'll reply to the email and set up a meeting.*

Rebecca: *Thanks. Let us know if you think it's worth all of us being on that call.*

As soon as you're a **subject of conversation** between two or three stakeholders inside a company, you have a much better chance of opening a door with them.

Because it's easy for someone to delete a one-way message. You send a message to Rebecca, she gets it, isn't interested, doesn't have time, hits delete: bang, you're dead!

But when Rebecca knows you've also contacted Ellen and Todd, now you're something that needs to be handled.

You have put yourself on the agenda because you've contacted more than one top dog.

And if you really want to get their attention when you email, make sure **they already know you.**

Or at least, make sure your name sounds somewhat familiar.

Here's how. Before you send out those emails to your C-suite targets, lay the groundwork by **"accidentally on purpose" connecting with them online and offline.**

As soon as you get the names, start liking their posts on LinkedIn. Start commenting, start sharing, start engaging in some meaningful dialogue on their social media.

Some might have a blog or a YouTube channel. Or they might contribute to the corporate blog. Hunt for their social media appearances, follow their posts and interactions, and be ready to leave an intelligent comment or share their post and tag them.

Do that first so that when you reach out to them, they'll feel that you're already an acquaintance.

Here's another way to be less of a stranger when you make that first contact to an executive: connect with a few lower-level people in their company first.

For example, on LinkedIn, before making a connection request to the CEO, make a few connection requests to folks in sales, marketing, or R&D. **Salespeople will almost always accept your connection.**

Then, after you've got 3–4 company contacts as connections, connect with your actual decision-makers.

This strategy is especially potent for LinkedIn because of the way LinkedIn works. LinkedIn tells the decision-makers you want to connect with that **you've got 4 mutual connections: two staff people and two salespeople.**

So, what do those decision-makers think?

This must be a client. This must be a prospect. This must be someone who's important because they're already connected to a few people on our team.

In other words, you're already in the family!

27 GATE OPENERS

Let's redefine this term right now: there are no gatekeepers in sales.

The same people you've been calling gatekeepers are actually gate openers.

Treat gate openers exactly like you treat your prospects.

Engage them in the sales conversation; engage them in the decision-making process.

Most other sales books tell you about avoiding or working around or minimizing contact with gatekeepers.

Would you want to avoid or work around or minimize contact with a gate opener?

Hmmmm...right, me neither.

And would you be kind, generous, and polite to a gate opener?

Or would you act like an arrogant jerk?

Too many consultants and experts have blown themselves up by being a jerk to the gate opener who they thought was "just the receptionist."

But it was the executive assistant to the president of the company.

And that executive assistant has the ear, respect, and attention of the president. Way more than you do.

Game over.

You are toast because you treated that person like a functionary or like someone to be avoided or worked around.

So always treat gate openers with respect.

Focus on including them, not excluding them.

Even if they have no role in the buying decision, assume they do, because it's a huge compliment to them.

Try something like this:

> Seller: *Who else besides you and Bob will make the decision?*
>
> Gate Opener: *No, no, I'm not involved in the decision.*
>
> Seller: *That's surprising. Doesn't he run things like this by you, just informally?*
>
> Gate Opener: *Well, yeah, you know, sometimes...*

If you want to send Bob a copy of your book, say this to the gate opener:

Let me send you two copies, one for you and one for Bob. Once you've taken a look and you think the company might benefit from those ideas, maybe we can get 15 minutes on Bob's calendar?

Notice the collaborative language highlighted in red. You, the company, we.

Treat gate openers the same as your prospects, because they ARE.

Gate openers are your friends.

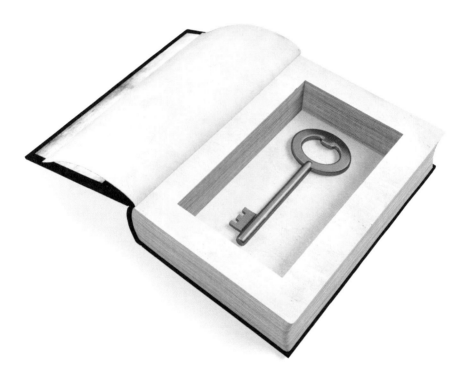

8

Initial Conversations

28 CAPTAIN, WE HAVE FIRST CONTACT!

Most prospect conversations start not as a sales conversation but as some sort of consultation call.

Your first contact will be a diagnostic call, audit, strategy session, discovery call, or exploratory chat.

Give this first consultation call a name so it conveys a sense of value.

For example, our initial consultation with prospects to help them define their next best steps to accelerate their consulting, coaching, or expert business is called a **Business Accelerator Call**.

If you'd like to experience one of these for yourself, simply go to **www.doitmarketing.com/call.**

You want to sell the value of the call, and that starts with the name.

If your expertise happens to be in e-commerce or career coaching or leadership consulting or innovation training or corporate strategy or presentation skills, consider the following names and naming conventions:

- E-Commerce Growth Call
- Career Breakthrough Session
- Leadership Strategy Session
- Innovation Accelerator Call
- Corporate Strategy Checkup
- Presentation Tune-Up Session

Beyond a name, it's important to have a structure for that first conversation.

A structure takes your prospects down a certain path of thinking.

For example, when you offer this call, tell prospects what they can expect and how the call flow typically goes.

When you go to a doctor's office, they sometimes just plop you down on the exam table, ask a few rote questions and start poking and prodding you.

Imagine if you went to a completely different kind of doctor who welcomes you in and says:

Here's the plan. First, we'll do a quick exam. We'll take your blood pressure. We'll get you on the scale. We'll look in your ears, up your nose, in your throat, all the usual stuff.

You mentioned you're having this cough. So we'll see what's going on there. Maybe a chest x-ray, maybe not. We'll figure that out.

And then we'll send you home with either some antibiotics if it's an infection or some pain reliever and cough drops if it's a plain old scratchy throat. How does that sound?

You feel calm because you know what's coming. You're more relaxed, and you like the doctor more because the uncertainty has been removed.

A smart salesperson has a process and tells you what that process is before she begins.

One of most powerful phrases to open a sales conversation is:

"Here's how I like to run these calls."

This phrase is not meant to be arrogant or condescending. It's the opposite. You're developing a partnership by sharing information and removing uncertainty.

Keep it short and tight:

During this consultation, we'll discuss:

1. *Where your business (or career or organization) is going.*
2. *Where you are currently.*
3. *Removing your [topic] roadblocks.*
4. *What other [buyer persona] like you have done to create success.*

No strings. No gimmicks. Just 2–3 smart ideas you can use right away to [main outcome], whether we decide there's a next step or not.

Just like that different kind of doctor, you're now a different kind of salesperson. You're letting your prospect know what to expect. You're making them feel at ease and more comfortable.

Which makes them feel like they're in the hands of a **true professional.**

To download a companion resource on this topic and grab ALL your free *Do It! Selling* templates, tools, and training videos, go to: **www.doitmarketing.com/selling**

29 5 TIPS FOR FIRST CONTACT CALLS

1. A great opening question

Because we work with owners of professional services firms, my first question during an initial conversation is always:

What have you done to get to where you are today? Give me a quick sketch of your professional journey up to this point. And then we'll spend the rest of the call on where you'd like to go next.

Why is that a great opener? Because prospects love talking, and they love hearing themselves talk. And their favorite subject is, of course, themselves.

The sooner in the sales conversation you get THEM talking, the more sales you will close.

2. "Do you mind if I treat you like a fee-paid client?"

This is another important phrase to use near the beginning of your calls.

Sometimes prospects will ask, "What does that mean?"

And my answer is:

That means I'm going to give you some specific advice. I may interrupt and redirect our conversation to maximize the value of our time, and I'll tell you what you need to hear and not necessarily what you want to hear. Is that OK with you?

Do you know how most prospects respond to this question?

Oh wow, that would be great. Yes, please. That's exactly what I want. I'm so confused. We're stuck with this problem...

3. Don't tell them about your smarts. Show them.

Deliver a powerful experience of value.

Make this a call they'll never forget.

Get real with them and hold up the mirror. Make them sweat.

Challenge their thinking. Bust some myths.

Rock the boat. Stir the pot.

Even better, share specific stories of similar clients you've helped and how those clients felt before, during, and after your work together.

Show them their own potential. Uncover the lies they've been telling themselves or their teams or their customers.

Let them have it exactly as if you just cashed their $50,000 check and this is your first meeting!

If you do that, their choice is not about, "Do I want to **hire** this expert?" but instead, "Oh my goodness, this was so VALUABLE! Do I want to **continue**?"

Once they've personally experienced the value you deliver, it's going to be much harder for them to want to stop.

Continuing becomes the only logical choice, doesn't it?

Treat prospects like clients, and you'll get a lot more clients!

4. The "Test-Drive" question

This is a question you need to ask at the end of every exploratory call:

> *"Bob, before we wrap up, I have one more question for you, and then I'm happy to answer any of your final questions. In my experience, two kinds of folks sign up for these*

consultations. The first group are folks who just want the free advice, insights, and guidance, and that's it. The second group are folks who want the free advice but who are also test-driving what a working relationship with me would feel like. Which group do you find yourself in?"

You'll be amazed because prospects will tell you the truth.

About 50 percent will say, "Nope, I'm good. I just wanted the free advice. Thank you so much."

A full 30 percent will freely tell you, "Yes, actually, I looked at your website and saw your LinkedIn profile, and we do actually need to hire some outside help in this area, so I am in test-drive mode."

What about the remaining 20 percent?

It's when someone says, "You know, I came on this call with no intention of buying anything or hiring you. After this conversation, though, I must tell you, I think we do need someone like you to help us, and I'd like to talk about what it might look like for us to work together."

Those are the best responses of all because they clearly prove that you totally rocked the consultation call!

5. Set up a separate call to maintain your sales integrity

A lot of salespeople make the mistake of selling on that initial exploratory call.

To me, that is a violation of the "prime directive" in the selling universe:

Never sell on a consultation call, and never do free consulting on a sales call.

That first conversation is truly a helping call, a consultation call, a diagnostic call, an exploratory call.

It's not a sales call.

Sales calls are earned, not assumed.

For those prospects who told you they are in "test-drive" mode, simply invite them to open their calendar right at the end of the helping call.

Here's what that might sound like:

"Great! I'm honored that you want to talk about what a working relationship might look like. Let me be clear: that was not the intention of this first call. I would never do a 'bait and switch' on you.

"This was purely a helping call and a consultation call, but because you're interested in working together, I'd be happy to set up a second call with you to discuss what we might do together. I've got Tuesday at 10 or Wednesday at 9:30. I'm on Eastern time. Which one of those works better for you?"

Once they agree to a time, send them a calendar invitation and a confirmation email with their preferred date and time in their own time zone.

The easier it is to book a sales call with you, the more sales calls you will book.

30 THE DREADED QUESTION

Has this happened to you?

You're talking to a prospect, and suddenly she asks you a question you've been dreading.

These questions typically sound like this:

- How many times have you done this kind of project?
- Have you worked with other clients in our exact industry?
- Can I talk to 10 other clients for whom you did this exact kind of work?
- Have you worked with companies of our size before?
- How many other nonprofit clients have you had?
- Do you specialize in working with companies like ours?
- Things work very differently in our industry. How well do you know it?
- We're in (location). Have you worked with clients here?

Fun fact: I once had a prospect tell me, "David, hang on. I don't think this will work for us. We're in Kentucky." I never found out what was so special about Kentucky, because my sales advice seems to work pretty well in the other 49 states (and around the world), but at least we now get to call ridiculous sales objections "The Kentucky Syndrome."

Depending on your own situation, background, and the particular prospect you're talking to, the "dreaded question" may vary.

In all cases, however, your immediate thought is:

Uh-oh, this is going to blow me up right now.

Why? Because there's no way you can answer that question truthfully without blowing up your chances of closing this sale.

In other words, you feel that YOUR answer is the WRONG answer and that this prospect just found you out.

I have good news for you.

There are always TWO right answers to the "Dreaded Question," and you need to find out which answer will resonate with your prospect.

"Wait, wait," I can hear you saying. "But, David, how can there possibly be two right answers? Are you saying I should lie to my prospects?"

The answer is absolutely not.

NEVER lie to prospects. There's already plenty of lying, deceiving, and evading on the prospect end of the equation. High-fee trusted advisors never add to it!

Perhaps you're familiar with debate competitions.

If you're not, here's the gist: They choose a controversial topic with plenty of factual background on both sides. The two debate teams are then randomly assigned to the "affirmative" (for) or "negative" (against) positions.

Note: this is regardless of their personal opinions and beliefs on the matter.

A skilled debater will be able to persuade equally well on EITHER side of the issue. That is exactly what they practice, and that is exactly how they win.

When most salespeople are asked "The Dreaded Question," they start squirming and tap-dancing. They fake it, they lie, and they delay. They start bobbing and weaving so much the prospect starts to get dizzy.

Remember the premise of a debate? Two sides, and either one can win. There's no ONE right answer or ONE right side. It depends on the skill of the debater!

When you're asked "The Dreaded Question," your best option is to be completely transparent: **openly acknowledge** this might be a deal breaker and immediately go into **debate mode.**

Let's say your "Dreaded Question" is, "Have you ever done a program like this for a big hospital or health-care system?"

Here's what that might sound like:

"Barbara, I have to be completely transparent with you. I'm afraid if I answer your question, I'm going to blow up this deal right now.

"You asked me if I have ever done a program like this for a big hospital or health-care system just like yours.

"Obviously, the answer you want to hear is, 'Yes, we've done dozens of them,' but that's not the case.

"We work with 2 kinds of clients. The first kind wants to stay firmly inside the hospital echo chamber.

"They only want to hear the same recycled cookie-cutter strategies, tactics, and training that all the other hospitals are using. Those tend to be the mediocre hospitals because no one ever won awards for following the herd and doing the same things every other hospital is doing.

"The second kind of client works with us specifically to get OUT of their own industry's echo chamber and discover a whole new world of best practices and proven tools so they can leap ahead, become more innovative, solve problems faster, and take a true leadership position among their peers.

"Which of those two best describes your thinking?"

Notice what just happened:

1. You became totally transparent and vulnerable.

2. You gave your prospect a new lens to rethink the premise of her "Dreaded Question," so now she's not so sure the answer she originally wanted to hear was the best answer after all.

Remember a time when someone was real with you and shared their inner fears and their inner dialogue. Did you think, *Wow, what a scheming, manipulative, evil person?*

Or did you think, *Wow, what a transparent, authentic, genuine person. I may or may not want to do business with him, but he's not the typical salesperson who lies, avoids, or squirms when faced with a tough question.*

This is a very advanced, rare, and sophisticated sales technique called:

Being completely truthful with prospects.

You unleash amazing selling powers if you go into every sales conversation with the guiding principle:

Nothing to fear. Nothing to hide.

Do that, and there will never be another "Dreaded Question" that you can't skillfully argue from either side of the "sales debate."

FORTUNE FAVORS THE BOLD

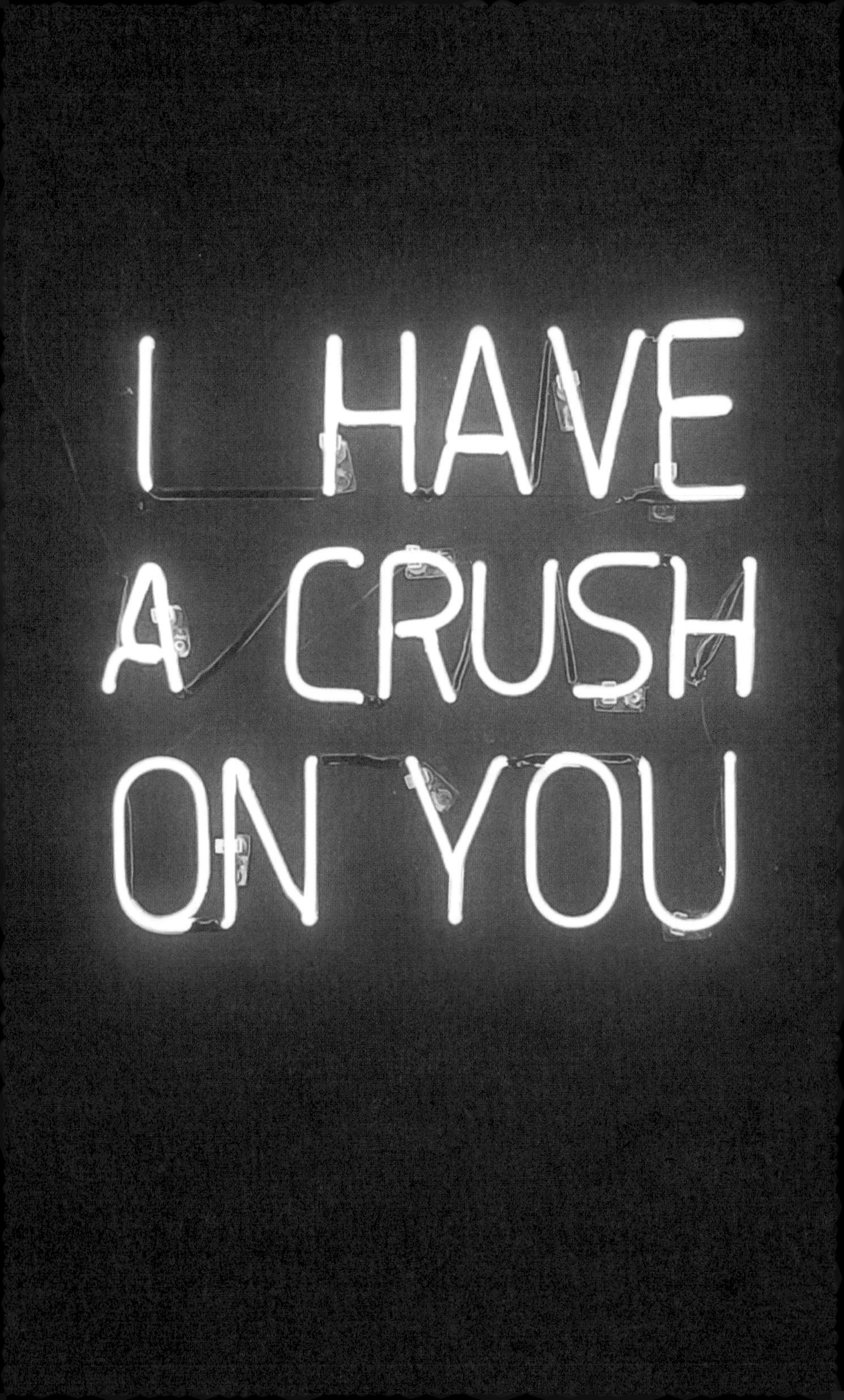
I HAVE
A CRUSH
ON YOU

9

Me without You

31 ME VS. YOU

Here's where a lot of professional services sellers make a huge mistake.

You sit down for a prospect meeting, and you are skewed toward way too much "ME" and not hardly enough "YOU."

- You ask trainer questions if you're a trainer.
- You ask coach questions if you're a coach.
- You ask consultant questions if you're a consultant.
- You ask speaker questions if you're professional speaker.

But you don't ask enough BUSINESS questions focused on them, their company, their team, their problems, their outcomes, and what they really want.

You don't ask, probe, dig, and uncover:

- What they're going through
- What their team wants
- What their CEO wants
- What their strategic initiatives are
- Why those initiatives are the strategic initiatives
- What their urgencies and priorities are
- What they're proud of
- What they're worried about
- What if it goes wrong?
- What if it goes right?
- Where they want to be in 90 days, 6 months, next year
- Why that's important to them
- How that impacts their numbers

- What those numbers mean specifically
- What are the radiant consequences of their problem?
- What are the radiant consequences of fixing their problem?
- What else is that going to impact?
- Who else?
- Where else?
- How else?

When you ask more questions, ask better questions, stay in the conversation longer, and take the conversation deeper, THEN and only then will you find out:

- The problem behind the problem
- The issue behind the issue
- The fear behind the fear
- The goal behind the goal
- The dream behind the dream

And that is exactly where the real money is hiding in every single sale you'll ever make!

32 THE SALES MIRROR

The best salespeople mirror their prospect's language.

And they feed back that language to anchor their points and move the sales conversation forward.

Prospects will literally SHOW you how to sell to them by using specific phrases, words, and vocabulary.

As sales guru Stew Bolno likes to say, "If they're talking about giraffes, oranges, and the number 17, you better not talk to them about monkeys, bananas, and the number 12!"

Use your prospect's exact words and phrases, which you'll hear and take note of, during every stage and phase of the sales process, from Zoom calls to follow-up emails to a written proposal, if you use proposals.

Phrases like "you mentioned," "you said you wanted," and "exactly as you described" open the door for repeating their exact words back to them in the context of your solution.

When they share specific problems, challenges, headaches, heartaches, gaps, hopes, dreams, goals, wishes, aspirations, and accomplishments, integrate those back into the conversation as you move through your sales process.

Here are some examples:

You're a career consultant, and your prospect wants to change companies and get a VP-level promotion. Do you want to close the deal with, "Let's get you into my whiz-bang career coaching program" or...

"Let's get you that VP job by this summer."

You're a marketing agency, and your prospect is an entrepreneur who's frustrated and stuck at the $150,000 per year income level. They really want to get to $300,000. Do you want to sign them up for your "digital marketing package #3" or...

"Let's create that $300K business for you."

During your conversation with an executive, you find out that she wants to send her oldest son to LSU because they're LSU football freaks. If this critical project hits all the milestones, she stands to earn a six-figure bonus.

"Let's lock in that LSU tuition for Charlie."

Your prospect is hungry for internal recognition and to get a proverbial "seat at the table" to increase their level of influence and status within their organization. You're helping them with project management consulting.

"Let's make this the project that gets your name in lights."

Vocabulary is vitally important.
Articulation is vitally important.
Specificity is vitally important.
To pick up that vocabulary, articulation, and specificity, all you have to do is LISTEN.

You don't need scripts. You don't need templates. You don't need to memorize any clever lines.

You just need to listen like your life depends on it.

And then feed back to your prospects exactly what they want, in terms that resonate with them, using exactly the same words they do.

All your sales conversations will be dramatically different from now on.

You'll sell more, more easily, and more often!

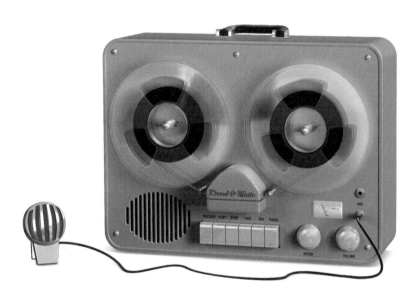

33 YOU'RE SAFE!

Here's a phrase that instantly relieves feelings of pressure for both prospects and for you. The words are simple, but the message is all-powerful:

Whether we decide there's a next step or not.

Throughout your sales conversations, keep using that phrase and ones like it.

- Whether we decide there's a next step or not
- If we end up working together in any capacity
- Should you decide you'd like to work together
- If we mutually decide this is a good fit
- Whether we ever talk again or not
- If this is something we eventually collaborate on or not
- We may or may not get the chance to work on this with you
- If we decide to move forward, this may be the first thing we tackle
- Whether we end up coming in to help you or not
- You might do this on your own or with a firm like ours at some future time

All these phrases engender something important that my friend Simon Bowen calls "buyer safety."

Think of these phrases as magic "get-out-of-jail-free" cards for your prospects.

They now know that it's perfectly OK if they end up not hiring you, not doing anything, or hiring someone else.

You are neutral like Switzerland. Cool like a cucumber. Unattached like a young George Clooney.

When you say, "Whether we decide there's a next step or not," and the other phrases listed above, you're really doing two things, both highly valuable for your sales success:

1. You're future pacing that at some point you will be asking for a decision.
2. You're making it totally safe for them to make that decision a "no."

Let's see this in action.

Prospect: "David, can you show us how to land large corporate consulting deals?"

Me: "Well, Susan, whether we decide to work together or not, the one thing I will tell you is that selling large corporate consulting deals is a little harder than it looks. But it's much easier than you've been making it. There are lots of improvements you can make, if this is something we eventually collaborate on or not."

What's happening there? I am talking to them like:

- A trusted advisor
- A friendly expert
- An authority
- An objective guide

Notice the tentative, conditional, pressure-free language, which shows I'm not a hungry dog going after red meat. I'm not going to come through the Zoom screen and grab them by the lapels and shake them until their cash and credit cards fall out!

Now maybe you're asking, **"Why should I give them an out?"**

Simple: To get your prospects to lower their shields.

Just like on the classic TV series *Star Trek*, all buyers have sales deflector shields. And when you start pitching and pushing and pressuring, those deflector shields go up, and the prospect hears the klaxons go off. It's "red alert" and battle stations!

But when you say things like, "Whether we decide there's a next step or not," "If we end up working together in any capacity," "Should you decide you'd like to work together," then their shields go down.

Because they're thinking, *Sounds like they're cool if we don't end up becoming a client. Sound like they don't really need our business. I'm not feeling that usual pressure I feel when I talk to other consultants*, so they relax.

If you're on Zoom, watch what happens when you start using these "buyer safety" phrases.

You'll see their body language soften. Their shoulders ease a little, and they start breathing a little more slowly. They relax.

What happens when a prospect is relaxed? They're a heck of a lot more excited about buying.

And that's exactly how you want your prospect to be.

Our job is not to sell.

Our job is to get them to step up so that they want to buy.

That's why this tentative or conditional language works so incredibly well.

If you always leave room for no, you create a lot more pull to yes.

10

Sell Faster, Sooner, Smarter

34 SELL THE DESTINATION, NOT THE TRANSPORTATION

Clients want outcomes, not inputs.

They want value, impact, and results. Not deliverables, models, methods, or "stuff."

It's not about the number of consulting sessions or about the number of coaching hours; it's not about "how many pages is the course binder we get?"

Selling works when it's 1,000 percent focused on what your prospect wants to do, achieve, solve, or become.

That's what you're selling: who they want to be, or where they want their company to be after you've left the building.

Describe that outcome in detail: the facts, the behaviors, the realities of what everything will look like once their problem is completely solved, or their outcome is fully realized.

What has changed? What is different? What will they see and hear that they don't see and hear now?

What observable behaviors have changed? What do their results look like?

Hard truth: nobody wants to pay for a consulting engagement or a coaching package or a seminar day.

No prospect ever wakes up and thinks, *I'd love to buy some consulting today.*

Instead, prospects want to invest in getting their personalized vision of a bigger, better, bolder future. And making that vision a reality faster with less work, less hassle, less risk, less fear, less uncertainty, and less doubt.

Selling the destination might be the only strategy you need to escape the price-driven sale.

You're no longer a commodity.

You're now a professional problem-solver.

Your expertise is no longer compared to dozens of other experts who do what you do.

You are now uniquely positioned as their trusted advisor.

And when you focus exclusively on their people, their problems, their team, their goals, their challenges, their obstacles, their results, their outcomes, and their future, that is when sales start to happen faster than you ever imagined possible.

Think of this another way. Your task is selling your prospect on a trip to Paris.

You can pitch this trip a couple of ways.

You can talk about how beautiful the Eiffel Tower is at dawn. You'll go out on your balcony as the sun rises behind the Arc de Triomphe, and you've got your fresh hot café au lait, and room service just delivered your still-warm chocolate croissants, and the person you love is looking at you adoringly over the chocolate croissants and says, "Honey, this is the most amazing, incredible vacation. You are the best partner ever. I love you. Let's get married."

That's one way to sell a trip to Paris.

Here's another way:

You are going to love this; we're flying to Paris on a Boeing 777-300ER.

This is way better than the Airbus A330, Airbus A340, McDonnell Douglas MD11, and the Airbus A350, and let me tell you why.

It has a range of 7,370 nautical miles, has a wingspan of almost 65 meters, and it runs on these amazing General Electric GE90-115BL engines with a maximum thrust of 115,000 pounds. Those bad boys have aerodynamically optimized fan blades in composite materials with titanium leading edges, plus a four-stage low-pressure compressor AND a nine-stage high-pressure compressor.

This thing is so awesome. It's got 396 seats. Oh, and the ailerons! This thing's ailerons blow away everyone else's ailerons. And did I tell you about the new semi-levered landing gear system? Total game changer! The unique gear, which is manufactured by Goodrich Corporation, allows the airplane to rotate early by shifting the center of rotation from the main axle to the aft axle of the three-axle landing gear truck.

We are going to have so much fun in Paris when we get there on this thing!

If you're thinking, "David, that's just plain dumb," I have bad news for you: This is probably how you sound to your prospects when you talk about your "stuff" instead of their outcomes.

The danger and temptation is when you ignore Paris, the Eiffel Tower, sunrise, your beautiful fiancé, the café au lait, and the croissants, and instead talk about the mechanics of the gosh darn plane.

No one cares about the plane. Everyone wants the romantic French getaway.

Sell the destination, not the transportation!

35 MULE VS. MAGICIAN

Which type of coach or consultant are you?

Mule or Magician?

There are two types of consultants.

A) The Mule

Those who sell their programs based on VOLUME of stuff.

Think pack mule: they love to load up!

If they charge $25,000 for their program, they believe they need to give

- Hundreds of pages of workbooks, manuals, and PDFs
- Tons of videos to watch, the longer, the better
- Endless hours of 1-on-1 and group coaching calls
- More and more content, webinars, ebooks, anything to make the program look "bigger"

B) The Magician

Those who sell their programs based on RESULTS clients get.

Where instead of volume, thick binders, and dozens of hours of videos...

Their #1 goal is to shorten the path and accelerate the speed at which clients achieve their goals.

There's a catch to this simple analogy:

Depending on which type of coach or consultant you are, that's the type of buyer you will be.

If you're the pack mule, all you care about is how big the binder is, how many coaching calls you get, how long the trainings are, and how many PDFs you get.

The more, the better. You love stuff.

DANGER: You're slowing down your clients and extending their time to results!

If you're the magician, it is all about results. How fast can I get to my outcome? Without having to read so much? Without having to spend countless hours watching videos?

Now the problem is:

If you're after more stuff, more PDFs, more videos, bigger downloads, bigger and heavier workbooks (the pack mule), you're NOT going to be successful.

Sad but true.

Every mentor's ethical responsibility is to shorten the path and accelerate the speed that a client gets to an outcome they want.

36 YOU CAN'T SERVE BIG IF YOU SELL SMALL

Biggest consulting deal of her career.

That's what the message said from one of our clients, a rockstar consultant who, a few short months before, had been struggling to the point where she almost threw in the towel on her business and went back to a corporate job.

I was so thrilled to read this message from her:

It's a $375K program, of which $300K goes to me.

One piece of advice I always give clients is:

You can't serve BIG if you sell SMALL.

Now, there's a subtlety to this advice...

Because we believe in magicians, not mules, serving BIG doesn't mean:

- Giving your clients bigger, thicker binders, workbooks, and slide decks
- Giving your clients endless training modules, videos, and classes
- Giving your clients more calls, more time, or more sessions

Remember: sales is all about THEM and all about THEIR OUTCOME.

Truly skilled consultants and experts **serve big** by asking themselves:

1) How can I shorten my clients' path to their desired outcome?

2) How can I accelerate my clients' speed to getting big results?

It's your ethical responsibility to make sure any meeting, training session, or resource is actually accomplishing those two goals for the greater good of your clients.

Don't give them stuff for the sake of stuff.

Don't give them more time for the sake of more time.

In fact, if you want to serve your clients even better...

STOP asking, "What can I **add** to my coaching or consulting offers?"

START asking, "What can I **remove** to help my clients get there even faster, with fewer detours, distractions, and speed bumps?"

37 CLARIFY, SPECIFY, AND QUANTIFY

It's not always easy to get your prospects to tell you EXACTLY what outcomes they're truly looking for.

Sometimes they don't even know themselves!

No worries.

Here are some of my favorite questions to help you clarify, specify, and quantify the tangible outcomes your future clients want.

Q: After our work together, what's happening then that's not happening now?

Q: What's new? What's different?

Q: What do you hear in the hallways?

Q: What are you hearing in your meetings?

Q: What's the back-channel buzz after we're done with this project?

Share your relevant client success stories to show them examples of what they are looking for.

You know, this reminds me of one of our other pharmaceutical clients. When they came to us, it was pretty much a carbon copy of what you just told me. Here's what she just sent me last week. Is it OK if I read an email to you? "I literally can't believe I work at the same company. Our culture has totally transformed. You wouldn't recognize this place from nine months ago."

Q: How do you see this ending up if all goes well?

Q: What would be a home run result for you?

Q: What does winning look like?

Q: What's one piece of tangible evidence you'd love to see?

A home run would be getting our voluntary turnover to less than 2 percent.

Winning means we become the #1 distributor in the US.

We'd get our top 20 spot back on Fortune's "100 Best Places to Work in America."

Q: What does success mean for you personally?

Well, personally, it would make me the local hero around here. We've been trying to tackle this all kinds of ways, and no one has been able to crack the code. It would make me feel great to have contributed to finally solving this problem.

Q: What does success mean for you professionally?

I'm hoping to get promoted one more time because I'm just five years away from retirement. I really want that SVP job, and our CEO said solving this is his top priority for the company.

Q: What does success mean for you financially?

I can't wait to have my stock options fully vested. And last year our bonuses were really light. This year I want to double my bonus, and a big part of that is based on hitting KPIs that this project will affect.

Q*: How would you describe your ultimate destination?

Help them paint the exact picture of their Eiffel Tower and their romantic sunrise breakfast with the love of their life.

Q: Can you put a number on it?

This is my favorite follow-up question.

Anytime someone gives you a vague complaint, unclear goal, or a squishy answer, ask them for specific numbers.

PROSPECT: *I'd like to see our retention numbers go up.*

YOU: *Where are they now? Where would you like them to be? Can you put a number on it?*

PROSPECT: *Our employee benefits costs are sky high.*

YOU: *What does "sky high" mean to you? Can you put a number on it?*

PROSPECT: *We want our defect rate to go down a notch or two.*

YOU: *Interesting! Can you put a number on it? What does "a notch or two" look like?*

In any sales conversation, never accept fuzzy, squishy answers!

To download a companion resource on this topic and grab ALL your free *Do It! Selling* templates, tools, and training videos, go to: **www.doitmarketing.com/selling**

11

It's Not Business, It's Personal

38 EMOTIONAL RESCUE

You're talking facts, figures, problems, challenges, goals, hopes, dreams, and you've sold the ultimate destination of what success looks like after your prospect invests in your brilliance.

That's great. Vitally important. Yet still intellectual.

We need to get emotional.

Because your prospects not only want those outcomes but they also crave the emotional payoff that comes with solving those problems and getting those results.

Listen closely to their language and put the emotional payoff they'll receive into the exact words and phrases they used earlier to describe their problems.

Common examples when my clients do this process with prospects include:

Confidence, clarity, control:
- Every senior executive and entrepreneur wants this.
- What words did your prospect use to describe their particular flavor of this desire?

Peace of mind:
- You leave for vacation, knowing that your team is doing all the right things, even when you're not watching.
- You wake up every morning feeling crystal clear on your goals and how they will move your department forward.
- You're no longer worried about gossip, gab, and the grapevine, and you've left the old office politics and turf wars in the rear-view mirror.

You're back in the driver's seat:
- You said you felt out of control. Imagine you're back in the driver's seat with every project you're responsible for.
- Let's get you back in the driver's seat so you're no longer feeling reactive, behind, and stressed out.
- Rather than a culture of "everyone for themselves," you're back in the driver's seat knowing you can overcome resistance and gain buy-in from your team effortlessly.

You're no longer overwhelmed:
- You're no longer overwhelmed by all the different demands on your time, and you move through your day feeling great.
- You mentioned all these conflicting priorities. Let's get you laser focused so you're no longer overwhelmed by all the complexity around here.
- Marketing can certainly feel like 100 extra jobs you hate. What if we simplified your marketing strategies so you're no longer overwhelmed and can get back to what you love, which is running your business?

You know exactly what to say and do:
- Conflict can be hard. Imagine if you knew exactly what to say and do in every difficult situation with colleagues, bosses, and your direct reports.
- When it comes to sales, there are a million ways a sale can go sideways. After working with us, you'll know exactly what to say and do at every stage of the sales process, from initial contact through signed contract.
- Performance reviews can be a legal minefield. With our system, you'll know exactly what to say and do at every

step to give an effective review, improve your team's results, and stay out of jail.

You'll know - You'll get - You'll have - You'll be - You'll feel - You'll do:
- You'll know exactly the type of clients you want to serve and where to find them.
- You'll get laser focused on how to invest your time, effort, energy, and priorities.
- You'll have the playbook so your whole team is in sync (like a boy band!)
- You'll be positioned as an expert.
- You'll feel extremely confident as your financial worries fade away.
- You'll do ONLY marketing tasks that you find easy, effortless, and enjoyable.
- You'll feel inspired, supported, and motivated to take action.

Use this emotional payoff language, and your prospects will start to think, *Holy smokes! This sounds amazing. Where have you been all my life?*

Because you're giving them exactly what they want, exactly what they need, in exactly the language they use to describe the problem.

39 THE NEGATIVE DETECTIVE

Yes, your clients are paying for their dreams. And the sooner you find out what those are, the sooner you can tailor your sales conversation around them.

But be careful because there's a trap here that most professional services sellers fall into. It's assigning YOUR meaning to THEIR words, commonly called "Happy Ears."

How do you fix that problem?

It's simple...

Never accept a dream at face value.

Dig deeper with these detective questions:

- So tell me why you want...?
- How would life be better?
- How would that benefit you?
- What options would you have then that you don't have now?
- What does that feel like?
- And so for you, that means...?
- Once you have that, what does that make possible?

Another way to surface some hidden motivations, urgencies, or buying triggers is to use these "Go Negative" questions:

- What if you don't do anything?
- What if nothing changes?
- What's the downside of that?
- That doesn't sound so bad. Wouldn't that be easier?

- What are the consequences?
- Don't these problems usually go away on their own?
- This isn't really your problem, though, is it?
- Won't someone else in the company swoop in and clean this up?
- Do you really have to get involved?
- You could probably live with the way things are if you had to, right?

When you go negative, they start to sell themselves (or resell themselves) on how horrible the problem is and how much they want to fix it.

12

Fearless, Shameless, Relentless

40 BE FEARLESS IN ASKING

During sales conversations, be fearless and relentless.

- Speak radical truths and be radically generous
- Do not back down
- Do not tread lightly
- Do not sound weak
- Do not worry about being liked

Do not hesitate to ask "delicate" or "sensitive" questions. If they cross your mind, ask them!

For example:

Based on the performance metrics that your boss has for you this year, do you have a personal financial interest in this project? In other words, if this project is successful, are you up for any kind of raise or promotion or bonus?

You may read that question and think, *Oh, that's about their money. That's too personal. I could never ask that question!*

Sure you could!

Because your "come-from" is in the right place.

You're not asking these questions to trap them or embarrass them or belittle them.

You're asking these questions because it's important diagnostic information you need to know so you can help them more deeply.

Do you have a personal financial interest in this project?

Answer 1: "This matters to my personal income not one bit."

Great. Now you know they are not personally invested in this outcome one way or the other. Some sales conversation options just closed for you, and some new ones opened up.

Answer 2: "They said they'll close our whole division in six months if we don't fix this."

Ding, ding, ding. Now you know they are personally invested in this outcome. And you have some more leverage plus some new areas of questioning to establish need, priorities, urgencies, and what it will take to make your buyer feel successful.

41 USE THE (SALES) FORCE!

In the second *Star Wars* film, *The Empire Strikes Back*, Yoda's pivotal advice to Luke Skywalker is to **"Use the Force**." Don't try to control your actions. Let the Force flow through you.

In a sales conversation, the Force looks like this:

The moment you want to say something or ask something during a sales conversation, you say it, you ask it.

When talking to prospects, listen to your "inner sales voice" that says things like:

- Wait, that doesn't make sense
- Hmmmm, that sorta sounds like BS
- Gosh, I have no idea what they're referring to
- That's a piece of jargon I don't know
- Wow, this is much worse than they think
- Hang on, a minute ago you said X, and now it's Y?
- Uh-oh, now they're just spewing buzzwords
- Sounds like someone is getting defensive
- We're going off track here
- What does that have to do with anything?
- There's only 7 minutes left and I haven't heard about their real problems yet

You know what voice I'm talking about, yes?

You need to remove the filter between sales brain and sales mouth.

This is a learned skill, and it's not easy, because two things usually get in the way:

1. Wanting to be liked
2. Wanting to sound smart

Let's tackle them one at a time.

First, wanting to be liked.

You have to let that go.

If you're talking to a good prospect, and you have highly relevant expertise to solve their problem or get them an outcome, don't worry about being liked. I'd rather have you make the sale. When you produce results for them, trust me, they'll like you!

On the other hand, if you're talking to a prospect who is easily irked or offended, doesn't tell you the truth, or gets evasive or weird, is that a client you really want to work with?

Second, wanting to sound smart.

The problem with wanting to sound smart is you think you need to understand everything the prospect says without questioning, probing, clarifying, or specifying.

A prospect might say, "We're working on improving our go-to-market strategies."

"Smart salesperson" response? **"Oh, great!"** Which means, "No need to say more. I'm supersmart and know exactly what you mean."

Truth is, you have no idea what the words **"working on"** or **"improving"** or **"go-to-market strategies"** mean to that particular prospect, in their context, with their problems, at that time, under their exact circumstances, with their specific stakeholders.

Dumb it down, Smarty-pants!

Do not try to sound "smart" on a sales call. Quite the opposite: **You need to be strategically dumb and perpetually curious.**

Strategically dumb means that you assume nothing. Stop pretending to be so darn smart. Stop accepting client and industry jargon or buzzwords in response to your questions. Stop accepting vague and squishy language when prospects try to minimize or ignore problems they're having. Keep asking what, why, how, who, when, and how much questions.

Perpetually curious means that you ask everything, and you ask a second, third, fourth, fifth, sixth, and seventh follow-up question to every initial question on your list. The key to higher fees and bigger deals is to ask better questions, ask deeper questions, stay in the conversation longer, and never be afraid to probe relentlessly for what's really going on.

When a prospect says, "We're working on improving our employee retention," that's the starting point to you asking 17 more questions.

Here are some questions that a strategically dumb and perpetually curious salesperson would ask:

1. Where's your retention today?
2. Where would you like it to be?
3. Where has it been in the past, when you were happy with it?
4. What makes you think your retention number is low?
5. What evidence do you have?
6. How long has retention been a problem?
7. What's that retention gap costing you in terms of dollars?
8. How does your retention stack up against peers and competitors?
9. What do you suppose your peers are doing about retention that you're not?

10. How is that affecting your own day-to-day work?
11. How is that affecting your team?
12. Has your CEO told you that fixing your retention is a priority?
13. Who else does this impact if retention doesn't improve?
14. Who wins if we fix the retention problem?
15. Who loses if we don't fix the retention problem?
16. How does fixing it, or not, affect you personally, professionally, or financially?
17. What if it's not fixable? Can you live with it where it is today?

Frankly, I was just getting warmed up, but I'll stop at 17 follow-up questions. You get the idea.

Secret tip: It's more like 51 follow-up questions because you can triple the number when you follow up on anything especially interesting, intriguing, or juicy with:

- **And what else?**
- **And where else?**
- **And who else?**
- **And how else?**
- **And why else?**

The best "sales script" is the one in your brain as you are listening, probing, asking, and uncovering in the moment based on exactly what your prospect is telling you.

Don't be afraid to tap into your intuitive inner salesperson.

When you use the (sales) Force, you are letting your "strategically dumb and perpetually curious" voice take over.

No prospect ever got mad at a salesperson for being too interested in them or asking too many questions about exactly what they want, what they need, what they're working on, why this is important to them, what they're trying to accomplish, or how they can be more successful.

But if you're focused on being liked or sounding smart, you'll do neither.

Nor will you close anywhere near the number of sales you deserve to win.

13

Sales Conversation Mastery

42 YOUR WITNESS, COUNSELOR

Every good sales conversation is built on questions.

Prospects will judge you far more on the quality of the questions you ask than on the statements you make.

You need to think like a courtroom attorney cross-examining a witness.

You don't just go in with a random list of questions; you go in with a questioning PLAN.

The plan is built on a sequence and syntax that walks the prospect through the thinking process YOU want them to experience.

And like every good courtroom attorney, you never ask a question you don't want the witness to hear themselves answer out loud in court!

Use your specific sequence of questions to lead the sales conversation down a path to reveal exactly what your prospect wants, why, when, how, how much, and how soon.

There are three cardinal rules of effective courtroom cross-examination.

RULE 1: ASK LEADING QUESTIONS

"I object! Leading question, Your Honor!"

If you're a fan of courtroom dramas on TV, you've heard that over and over.

The reason leading questions are objectionable is because they contain some or all of the answers a lawyer seeks from a witness.

In other words, you are trying to put words into your prospect's mouth.

The trick is to use leading questions without them feeling like leading questions.

For example, if you're probing for timing, urgency, and priority, here's **what NOT to do:**

I suppose this project is urgent for you, right?

My guess is you want to solve this fast, don't you?

Most of our clients want to stop the bleeding ASAP. Do you feel the same?

Here's how to do it:

What's your time frame for getting a fix in place?

How much longer are you willing to put up with what you've described?

Where is this on your strategic priority list overall?

RULE 2: ASK ONE NEW FACT PER QUESTION

Often, you'll fall into the bad habit of stacking your questions.

This mashes together 3 to 4 questions into what sounds like a single question, and your prospect loses focus and often ends up giving you less information on all parts of your question.

Here's an example:

How long has this been a problem, where else is this showing up, and who else is involved?

That's three questions all stacked into one.

This is bad, and here's why:

You are wasting ammunition. You just used up three questions to move the person one step forward...or backward.

You're not giving them space to answer in depth. Chances are, they'll pick the one question they have a good answer for, and your other two questions will be forgotten.

You sound nervous, inexperienced, or both. Rather than rush through a list of stock questions, you want your prospect to feel that you are fully present, fully listening, and fully committed to tailor a perfect solution to their exact problems.

Effective sales questioning can be like playing chess. Different answers might send you to completely different squares on the board. You make your next move based on their previous move.

Your job is to stay responsive, open, and pay close attention to what they say, how they say it, and what they leave unsaid.

Listen carefully to every answer. Only when that answer is completely fleshed out should you move on to the next question.

RULE 3: QUESTIONS MUST FOLLOW A LOGICAL PROGRESSION TO EACH SPECIFIC GOAL

We're talking about your specific sales goals.

What do you need to know? What do you want to find out?

Don't ask random questions in random order.

When you do that, prospects feel you're disorganized, ignorant, or following some sort of robotic script.

This is about sales syntax. What comes logically first, second, third; and what makes no sense to ask before something else was established first.

The absolute worst kind of sales conversation sounds like an interrogation because it's a series of random questions asked sharply with zero acknowledgment of the questions or answers that have come before.

If you've ever been on the receiving end of a sales interrogation, you know how weird, frustrating, and nerve-grating it can be.

Your prospect immediately goes into "how soon can I make up an excuse to get off this call?" mode.

Every question you ask should be a logical step forward that builds the case in the prospect's mind of why they want what you do, why they need what you do, and how buying from you **solves all the problems and creates all the outcomes** that are near and dear to their hearts.

43 OH, HMMMM, GOSH

Imagine you're in the doctor's office.

The doctor is looking at your x-ray, points his finger to a gray hazy spot on your lung, and quietly mutters:

Oh.

What's your reaction?

Probably not this: *Hey, Doc, relax. My lung is fine. Trust me. I feel like a million bucks. Don't you worry about that little gray spot.*

Your reaction is probably more like this:

Oh my God. I'm going to die. It's all over. I'm gonna lose that lung. Doc, what do you see? What are you pointing to? What the hell is it?

After all, the doctor is the expert, the authority, your trusted advisor on medical issues.

When the doctor quietly mutters, "Oh," you pay attention!

When you, the expert, the authority in your field, mutters, "Oh," your prospects will have the same reaction: **they start to pay attention.**

Which gives you the opportunity to ask more questions, deeper questions, better questions, and stay in the conversation longer.

Because sometimes the most powerful follow-up questions are literally muttered under your breath.

Oh is a good start.

You've also got:

- *Hmmmm*
- *Gosh*
- *Wow*
- *Ugh*

- *Hoo boy*
- *Really?*
- *Terrible*
- *Unbelievable*

- *That sounds bad*
- *Geez*
- *Whew*
- *Yikes*
- *No!*
- *Ouch*
- *C'mon, really?*
- *You're kidding*
- *That bad?*

Muttering any one of these phrases quietly will open up your prospect to say more, elaborate in more detail, or go deeper into what they were just telling you.

44 NOW, NOW, NOW

Are you anchoring your sales conversations in the now?

If not, you're making it far too easy for prospects to delay, procrastinate, and tell you they will buy later.

In sales, later means never.

You've probably heard these two pieces of sales wisdom:

Money loves speed.
Time kills deals.

Both are profoundly true.

When it comes to sales, NOW is money.

But how do you shift your prospect into the gear of NOW?

Here are four important reasons you need your prospect to be thinking in NOW mode:

1. You're going to help them **set up correct beliefs based on facts**. You'll help them see the reality of what's going on and get to the underlying truth of their situation, including the good, the bad, and the ugly of their current state.

2. You're going to help them **destroy false beliefs** that are based on wishful thinking, arrogance, complacency, self-soothing delusions, corporate ego, or lies they've been telling themselves to keep them safe. Because it's not keeping them safe. It's keeping them stuck. It's keeping them spinning their wheels and not getting results.

3. You're going to help them uncover their own sense of **genuine urgency** based on their specific situation, their

goals, their time lines, their priorities, and what they're going through in the present moment.

4. You're going to **enforce consistency** because prospects usually don't disagree with their own statements. Early in the sales conversation, when you ask about their deadlines, their project dates, and any other time-bound restrictions or goals they have, it becomes much harder for them to tell you, "This is a bad time," or "We don't have the time for this project."

Get them to NOW early so that later, there's nowhere to hide.

It's hard for them to argue with:

Because you said you want these results by the end of Q2.

Because you said if you don't fix this now, it's only going to get worse.

Because you said your CEO wants this done before the board meeting.

Here is your starter set of questions to get your prospect thinking and talking in NOW mode:

- What's not working in your business right now?
- What made you book this call now?
- Why is now the time to fix this?
- What's important about that now?
- Why is this a priority right now?
- What happens if you don't fix this now?
- Did someone urge you to look into this now?

Throughout your sales conversations, keep your ears open for additional opportunities to insert NOW mode questions, such as:

- If you had that going now, what would that mean to you?
- Because you don't have that now, what problems is that causing?
- Because you're not doing that now, what's that costing you?
- If you could fix that now, what would that mean as far as results?

Another way to get to the heart of urgency is to ask time-based questions like these, including questions that **test their urgency** by bringing up the idea of waiting:

- How much longer are you willing to put up with X, Y, and Z problem?
- How soon would you like to start to generate A, B, and C results?
- Are you sure you want to fix this now?
- Why not wait a few months?
- Why is now the best time to put in all this work to make that happen?
- What might prevent you from fixing this now?
- If this is so urgent, why hasn't it been fixed before now?

Keeping your prospect in NOW mode is one of the keys to help you unlock better clients, bigger deals, and higher fees.

Once you start practicing these question-based, deep-dive, high-integrity sales conversations, you'll become far more effective at uncovering, discovering, probing, agitating, expanding, and revealing the truth of what's going on with every prospect you talk to.

It will also help you cut through the corporate ego, remove self-soothing delusions, defuse arrogance, confront complacency, bust through myths, and prevent many of the most common objections (before they ever come up) that stand in the way of you making the sale.

How do you like me now?

To download a companion resource on this topic and grab ALL your free *Do It! Selling* templates, tools, and training videos, go to: **www.doitmarketing.com/selling**

45 DON'T BE BLINDSIDED

Your sales process is zooming ahead when suddenly...

- *"I gotta run this by the committee before we sign."*
- *"We can't do anything until the big board meeting."*
- *"Our VP needs to approve this. And she hates consultants."*

Nobody likes to be blindsided.

You do not want any surprises coming from their end.

And they don't want surprises coming from you.

Each surprise, each unexpected twist, can add to your sales process anywhere from a week to a month.

And you don't want that.

The best way to prevent surprises is to ask key buying questions early on in your conversations and throughout at every major step and milestone.

If you want to instantly sell more, find out right away HOW this prospect is going to buy!

Start with no-frills, direct questions about their buying process:

1. If you were to decide this is a good idea, how do you buy things like this?
2. How do you implement?
3. What should I know about your timing? Sign-offs?
4. When do you budget for things like this?
5. Do you think this deal is going to work?
6. What's missing or what should we add?
7. Are you going to pitch it?
8. What else do you need to see from me?

9. Can I help you put together some numbers?
10. Do you have some numbers I could include?

The next set of questions is for **multiple-buyer situations.**

11. Who else besides you will be making this decision?
12. Are they going to like it?
13. WHAT are they going to like?
14. WHAT are they going to push back on?
15. What else is going to be in our way?
16. How would YOU respond to that?
17. What answers do you need from me so you're prepared to answer their questions?
18. How much detail do YOU want?
19. How much detail will THEY want?
20. Are there any surprises we should be prepared for?
21. If this were just you and me, how excited would you be to move ahead on a scale of 0–10?

Hint: If they answer 9 or 10, you're good. If they answer 7 or 8, ask, "What would need to change to get us closer to 10?" If they answer 6 or less, you have a problem. Go for no with "I don't think we can make this work. Do you?"

Bonus idea: In his book *To Sell Is Human*, Dan Pink offers this brilliant advice for any answer below 8: Ask the opposite question. "Seven? Interesting. I'm curious why you didn't choose a **lower** number? Why isn't it a 5 or a 2?" Watch the prospect now start to resell themselves on why working with you is important, urgent, relevant, and useful.

Be relentless and follow up like a friendly bulldog.

Never let an active prospect get more than 5 days away from you.

Always show up in their world like a happy, squeaky wheel: Send more value. Ask more questions. Offer more engagement. Invite further dialogue. Come back with more ideas to genuinely help them.

More and better and faster sales will follow.

46 SALES CONVERSATION ROADMAP

Here is the sequence of questions that will get all your sales conversations on track and keep them on track.

1. **What are your three biggest [topic] strengths and three biggest [topic] challenges?**

If your professional services have to do with improving customer service, for example, this might sound like:

What are your three biggest customer service strengths?
What are your three biggest customer service challenges?

Why start with strengths?

Because prospects have egos, they have pride, and they like to brag.

No one likes to start by admitting weaknesses, so consider this the "warm-up round."

What's the thing they love most after bragging? Complaining, of course! And their pet peeves. And venting their frustrations.

In the process, they're presenting a broad spectrum of issues you can then probe around, uncover more details about, and dig further into.

The next series of questions gives your prospect the feeling they've already started working with you and benefiting from your insights before any money has changed hands:

2. **Pretend we're starting our work. What's the first thing you'd want to ask me?**

3. **What would we tackle next?**

4. **If accepted, what specifically are you hoping to gain from our work together?**

(Notice that language. Like Harvard, Yale, and Stanford, we're taking applications and being highly selective in accepting clients. Subtle but incredibly effective!)

5. **What does success look like? Where do you see yourself after 90 days working with us?**

This is where the rubber meets the road.

You think you know what your client's success looks like, but that doesn't matter. We need to get crystal clear on what THEIR definition of success looks like.

And we need to manage expectations about where things might be in 90 days.

If they start painting a picture of complete top-to-bottom transformation in 90 days, and you know it usually takes even your best clients 3 years to attain that level of success, now is the time to reset those expectations and possibly expand the scope, scale, and duration of your initial project to the tune of a 50 to 500 percent increase in fees.

6. **What's new? What's happening then that's not happening now?**

Here's the magic in this set of questions: they are now visualizing what they want to work on with you, what outcomes they would (finally) get, and what problems they would (finally) solve.

Probe for details here once they start talking.

Ask follow-up questions such as:

- And what else?
- What else would happen after that?
- And from there, what becomes possible?
- Who else is impacted by that change?
- And who else?
- Where else in the company might that have a positive impact?
- And where else?
- How else might that be a benefit to you or the department or the team or the organization as a whole?
- And how else?

This is also the time to share specific success stories, case studies, and directly comparable clients and projects.

Make your prospect feel they're in familiar territory and that you've solved similar problems for similar clients in similar situations under similar conditions.

14

Engage!

47 NO MORE DANCING MONKEYS

Do you do sales TO your prospects?

Or do you do sales WITH your prospects?

That's a trick question (Gotcha!)

When we do sales TO our prospects, it's about as effective as putting on a dancing-monkey show.

Maybe the audience claps. Maybe they throw you a peanut. Maybe they walk away.

They're a passive observer, and it may or may not interest them.

Clearly, there's a better way.

When you do sales WITH your prospects, it's a collaborative process, and both parties are actively engaged.

How do you get prospects to actively engage in your sales process?

Put them to work.

Condition your prospects to **respond** to you from the start.

- Send them a questionnaire to answer
- Send them a one-page worksheet to complete
- Send them a pre-call video to watch
- Send them an application form
- Send them a self-assessment
- Send them a PDF to read
- Send them a survey

Send them anything that will require them to **DO something**!

If they take action, they are no longer passive observers watching the show.

If they submit the questionnaire or return the completed worksheet, they are now actively involved in the sales dialogue with you.

They're your collaborators and your partners. Meaning, you are now **peers**.

Send them something to do before and in between every significant step in your sales process, and they will be fully engaged throughout.

Fully engaged prospects are much more likely to become fully committed clients.

**INVOLVEMENT leads to ENGAGEMENT
leads to COMMITMENT.**

48 PRE-WORK TO PRE-QUALIFY

What if prospects don't engage with your pre-call sales assignment?

They just did you a favor.

They showed you they're not serious.

They saved you from wasting time on a non-prospect.

You will never get a serious prospect who is not willing to do the pre-work.

Let's say you send them a pre-call video and a quiz. That's what we do with prospects who are interested in our Do It! MBA revenue acceleration mentorship.

If they complete the quiz, they've already become engaged in the MBA mentorship because they've actively taken a step forward.

When I get on a Zoom call with a prospect, the first question I ask is, "Did you get a chance to watch the video?"

Our best prospects answer with some version of "Yes, of course I did. When I saw the email asking me to watch it, I actually watched it twice."

Cool.

Chances are excellent this is a good prospect and someone we would love to help.

But if they weren't willing to do three to four minutes of work, or watch a short video, then I know they are not a serious prospect.

Great prospects buy your sales process before they buy your services.

It's the sale before the sale and it's a great filtering and sorting mechanism.

Use pre-work to pre-qualify your prospects.

More prospect engagement will lead you to more client engagements!

15

The Clients You Don't Want

49 7 STUPID WAYS TO BLOW UP YOUR SALES PROCESS

 Let me tell you about the WORST sales call of my life, and all the red flags I chose to ignore.

After reading this, YOU can apply these seven lessons to YOUR sales process so you never have to blow it like I did.

1. Wrong prospect. I knew it in my bones even before we got on the phone. He doesn't fit; he's missing many of the qualities, traits, and characteristics of our most successful clients; and he's sort of an "odd duck."

2. Wrong process. Did he read the material I sent ahead of time? No. Did he know what business we are in? No. Did he understand how we work, and what we do, and why? No. Is this my prospect's fault? HELL NO! It's my fault for not following my own process (and not making sure the prospect followed it too). The only thing worse than "wrong process" is NO PROCESS. And I've been guilty of that in the past as well, but this time it was all on me that **I had a process that my prospect did not follow.** I should have rescheduled the moment I found this out. But I didn't.

3. Wrong budget. Why, why, WHY do you keep having sales conversations with people whose initial inquiries start with the phrase "money is tight" or "our budget's been cut" or "I don't have two nickels to rub together" (I've gotten all three of these verbatim dozens of times. And usually I know what to do.) If they claim poverty on the approach, they will not suddenly become millionaires on the call. **Bring up money FAST and EARLY.** Not your fees but THEIR own pricing, THEIR ROI, THEIR average sale, THEIR customer lifetime value. Do that and you'll set the **context** for your fees as an investment, and you'll be able to **avoid the sticker shock** when you drop a number on someone before you've established commensurate VALUE for them.

4. Wrong words. Do you listen (TRULY listen) to what your prospects say in the first few minutes of your sales conversations? Can you identify when they are using the "right words" versus the "wrong words" to indicate their readiness to move ahead, their understanding of the value that your products and services bring, and their level of sophistication as an educated consumer? If you did, **you'd make more sales faster**, and you'd stop wasting precious selling time with price shoppers, tire kickers, and broke-ass losers.

5. Wrong questions. Do you listen just as carefully (maybe more so) to the kinds of questions your prospect asks YOU during the sales call? Can you tell from THEIR questions if they are modeling your best clients and customers? Can you identify their underlying urgencies and priorities based on the questions they ask? Have you ever **gently redirected a "bad" question** with the phrase, "The real question I'm hearing you ask is…" "And the answer to that question is…" Examples of bad questions include fear-based questions that fixate on guarantees, warrantees, all that could go wrong, insignificant details, and irrelevant metrics.

6. Wrong bravado. When a prospect spends any significant amount of time telling me how successful they are, how financially lucrative their business is, how much money they make, and what kind of car they drive, I know we're not a fit. Here's the truth, folks: **Successful people ARE successful. They don't need to TALK about being successful.** Someone who brags like this probably suffers from low self-esteem or, even worse, is a mental child who still needs to impress mommy and daddy who never loved them enough in the first place. Move on. And fast!

7. Wrong fit. Put your current prospect in an imaginary lineup with your very best clients, both past and present. Does this prospect fit? Do they belong there? Are they a natural extension of your business family? If not, that should be enough to get you to hang up the phone right then and there. **Like attracts like.** If your prospect would stick out like a sore thumb in your lineup of great clients, that means there is something seriously wrong. DO NOT allow that prospect into the circle of the clients whom you love working with and who love you.

Fail to heed these seven warning signs and **the best-case scenario** is that you'll waste a lot of precious time, energy, and effort on the wrong prospects who will never do business with you anyway.

And **the worst-case scenario** is that you'll end up with a goofball client, or at the very worst, a "nightmare client from hell."

50 NO SOUP FOR YOU!

The key to great selling is great clients.

Remember the mantra I shared back in Chapter 24: the better you are at client selection, the worse you can be at everything else.

Make sure to disqualify early.

Just like the "Soup Nazi" character on *Seinfeld*, I would encourage you to be choosy about who you want to do business with and who you do not.

He would regularly throw customers who annoyed him out of his shop with the phrase "No soup for you! Come back in ONE YEAR!"

You want the right prospects to talk to and you ONLY want to talk to the right prospects.

Sales is NOT a numbers game.
It's a value game, it's a relationship
game, and it's a relevance game.

Don't let any sales training idiot tell you it's a numbers game. That's pure lunacy.

As soon as possible, get the tire kickers, the price shoppers, and the non-decision-makers **out of your world**!

Get them off your calendar. Remove, delete, block, ban.

51 LET'S GET REAL OR LET'S NOT PLAY

One of the bonus benefits of having a structured sales process in place is that you can tell when your sales process (or your prospect) is GOING OFF THE RAILS.

- You can tell when something is starting to slip...
- Something's starting to go sideways...
- The client's about to go dark on you...
- You're dealing with a tire kicker, a price shopper, or a goofball who's wasting your time...

And at that point, your attitude needs to be:

Let's get real or let's not play.

That happens to be the title of a great sales book from 1999 by Mahan Khalsa.

But it's also a great sales philosophy for dealing with prospects who are:

- Not treating you with respect
- Not showing up for your scheduled calls
- Not answering your emails
- Not telling you the truth
- Not willing to share information you need
- Not committed to solving their own problem
- Not serious about getting the results they talk about

Whether it's prospects or partners, remember this wise relationship advice:

If the dating doesn't go well, it won't get better once you're married.

52 LOSE THE JOKERS

Anytime you start to get the feeling that a prospect is not serious, playing games with you, or simply stalling, avoiding, dodging... it's time to **lose the jokers.**

The person who brings up NO first usually wins, and I want that to be YOU!

Why would you want to blow up your own sale?

Because with prospects like this, you're probably going to lose the sale anyway.

When you get out the dynamite and light the fuse under a problematic prospect's chair, you're saving yourself from wasting tons of sales time and sales energy.

And sometimes you might even turn the sale around by showing you're willing to walk away.

When you're not afraid to lose the sale, you can be totally transparent and direct, and you can call them on their obfuscation (a.k.a. BS).

Here's your "Lose the Jokers" phrase book to help you sort out serious buyers from the tire kickers, price shoppers, and time wasters:

- It sounds like it really doesn't make sense for you to solve this problem.
- So this is not a problem you're looking to solve right now, is it?
- I'm sorry. I'm confused. Help me understand...
- Do you want to solve this problem or just talk about solving it?

- Seems that you're 100 percent OK not doing anything about this right now. Am I correct?
- Be brutally honest with me: This is never going to happen, is it?
- I can't find a single reason for us to do business. Can you?

However you decide to respond, remember the guiding principle of:

Nothing to fear. Nothing to hide.

If your prospect blows up right then, I have good news: You were never going to win that sale anyway. And you've saved potentially weeks or months of chasing a nonbuyer.

More good news: you really dodged a bullet because **they would've been a terrible client anyway!**

That's the flip side of "You're not going to WIN them all," which is "You're not going to WANT them all."

Nightmare prospects who need to be chased, convinced, persuaded, cajoled, and begged rarely make good clients.

Don't be afraid to lose the jokers.

You can never want the sale more than they want the solution.

Don't worry about the RIGHT prospects saying NO. Worry much more about the WRONG prospects saying YES.

53 5 SIGNS YOUR PROSPECT IS GIVING YOU TOO MUCH BS

Your prospecting and sales process should be easy, effortless, and enjoyable.

Period. End of sentence.

If it is not, and if you're attracting difficult, high-maintenance, or unenjoyable prospects, here's another sales adage for you:

Sometimes the best deals are the ones you don't do.

Here are 5 signs you're dealing with a bad prospect, and your best option is to run away FAST:

1. Agreeing to sign on and then backing off at the last minute or the next day to ask for references, birth certificates, blood tests, or guarantees.

2. Bargaining and asking for price reductions with no corresponding reductions in services, terms, value, or relationship (Asking for a price concession "just because" is a classic form of prospect BS!)

3. Undervaluing your services, track record, and expertise. "I could do this myself; I just don't have time..." or "We've outsourced this to several vendors and have never been happy..." (Run, my friend! Run!)

4. Telling you up front, "We're notoriously difficult to work with / a control freak / a perfectionist / highly demanding / but don't take it personally." (This means they've been fired by other service providers in the past, and they're prepping you for the same

eventuality while playing BOTH sides of "good cop / bad cop." Nice!)

5. Using terms of false affection, like "Big Guy" and "My dear," or false compliments, like "You are a great salesperson!" (Obviously, if you were a great salesperson, you would not be wasting your time with this narcissistic sociopath nightmare client from hell, would you?)

As poet Maya Angelou so eloquently said:
"When someone SHOWS you who they are, believe them."

54 YOUR NINE-POINT CLIENT GPS

GPS, in this particular case, stands for Goofball Prevention Screening, and here's why you need one.

Every day here at Do It! Marketing HQ, we work hard to make sure the clients we love are extremely happy with their progress and their results.

We also work hard to keep OUT clients who will make us nuts, sap our energy, or with whom it's impossible to do our best work.

In this spirit, here is an example to model if you'd like to create your firm's very own client GPS.

A client may well prove to be a goofball if they...

1. Lack high standards of excellence. Good enough is good enough...

2. Don't care about increasing their knowledge. Not committed to becoming valuable resources to their own clients and customers...

3. Refuse to work hard and commit to their own success. Lack persistence and unwilling to try new things to achieve results...

4. Think they already know everything. And they resist advice on expanding their skills, expertise, or capabilities...

5. Reluctant to invest in themselves and their business. They fail to understand that this is the best investment of all...

6. Operate from a mindset of fear and scarcity. They can't make good long-term decisions, because they are so risk-averse in the short term...

7. Won't (or can't) pay their bills. Their lack of financial responsibility spills over onto others in the form of late payment, non-payment, and endless excuses...

8. Exude negative energy. Negative self-talk, pessimism, and cynicism repel new opportunities, new partners, and new ideas (all vital to success)...

9. Can't commit to mutually supportive relationships. In business and in life, the most successful people don't go it alone...

That's my list. Are you ready? It's YOUR turn...
A client may well prove to be a goofball if they...

1. _____

_____

2. _____

_____

3. _____

_____

4. _____

_____

5. _____

_____

6. _____

_____

7. _____

_____

8. _____

_____

9. _____

_____

To download this exercise in electronic form and grab
all your free *Do It! Selling* templates, tools, and training
videos, go to **www.doitmarketing.com/selling**

55 YOU CAN'T BLOW UP A GOOD PROSPECT

Years ago, I got a call from a gentleman named Carlos.

Here's how he started our first conversation when he called me:

David, I've been following you for a while. You're my guy. I'm about to leave my corporate job, and I want to hire you as my marketing coach.

I asked Carlos what kind of company he wanted to start.

I'm starting three different businesses. One is a talent development company. And a recruiting firm. And I'm also building a consulting practice for HR leaders.

I told Carlos that each of those companies are multibillion-dollar industries on their own, and I felt he was biting off way more than he could chew.

Building a successful consulting business in any ONE of those three areas would be hard enough, let alone trying to push three boulders uphill at once!

Then I drew the line in the sand and told him, "I feel there's no way you can be successful if you're hell-bent on doing all three of these businesses. For that reason, I can't work with you. But I sure appreciate you calling me up."

We ended the call, and I figured I would never hear from Carlos again.

Remember: He practically had a credit card in hand. He told me, "I want to hire you. You're my guy."

And I turned him down.

I said, "Nope. We're not doing this. You will not be successful."

To quote from the sharks on *Shark Tank*, "And for that reason, I'm out."

But the story doesn't end there, because Carlos called me back the next day.

David, I've been thinking pretty much all day yesterday and today about what you said. And you're right. There's no way I'm going to be focused. There's no way I'm going to be successful. I'm not going to do the recruiting firm. I'm dropping the HR consulting idea. But I really do want to start a talent development company. That's my sole focus. And I'd like you to be my marketing coach.

That day Carlos became a client. And we did some great work together.

The lesson?

There is nothing you can say that will blow up a good prospect.

Including, "No, I don't want to work with you."

If you DO say something, and the prospect goes ballistic or gets offended, starts to argue or insult you, or disappears on you, guess what? They were NEVER a good prospect to begin with, and you just did yourself a huge favor and found out early.

Carlos was a good prospect and a great client.

Because I didn't sugarcoat my advice and showed him that I was more committed to his success than to grabbing his credit card, he became a client.

Even though I turned him away.

Let's face it: sometimes those nightmare prospects from hell do show up, and it's your job to turn them away.

Listen to that little voice in your head that sometimes warns you, "Uh-oh, this sounds like a high-maintenance client, this sounds like trouble, we have some crazy-making behaviors brewing, danger, danger!"

Here's the magic of what happens next...

How many times have you fired a terrible prospect or a terrible client, and within 24 to 48 hours **a totally amazing prospect shows up, buys from you, and replaces them?**

When you develop the strength and insight to fire bad prospects early, the universe compensates and sends you an amazing replacement almost right away.

Based on our work with over 1,800 consultants, coaches, and experts, this apparently happens quite regularly.

I bet it's happened to YOU. Probably more than once, right?

16

F.U.

56 HOW TO AVOID DISAPPEARING PROSPECTS

Relax! This section title stands for "Follow Up" (I don't know what YOU were thinking!)

Let's start by curing the deadly sales disease known as "DPS" or Disappearing Prospect Syndrome.

Don't you hate that?

Do you know why it happens, at least most of the time?

There are countless surveys of executive decision-makers, including C-level executives at small- and medium-sized companies, and VP-level buyers at larger companies where they've asked, "Why do you engage with a salesperson or consultant?"

The #1 answer across the board is "to learn something new" or "get insights about my industry, updates on issues important to our company, tap into emerging trends, and learn what my competitors are planning or doing that I am not."

Thus, it's natural to conclude that when you STOP sharing insights with your prospects, that is the exact moment there is no longer any value to them in engaging with you, and they stop responding to your calls, emails, and messages.

After all, how compelling and exciting are questions like "Are you ready to buy yet? How about now? Maybe now? OR how's right now?"

Makes perfect sense, right?

Would you reply to any of those pestering follow-ups?

Right, I wouldn't either!

How do you keep the insights and value flowing from initial contact through signed contract?

NEVER stop sharing valuable insights, useable intelligence, and contrarian or counterintuitive ideas with your prospects!

The best way to keep a sales process moving forward is to have a set of value items already prepared so that you're never just following up for no reason.

With every follow-up touchpoint, you're adding value.

You're sharing a resource, or you're being helpful.

The best way to get that going is to collect your 5 or 10 value items ahead of time so they are at your fingertips and ready to deploy.

Some of these value items could be yours, and some might be from sources like *Harvard Business Review*, *Forbes*, *Fast Company*, some YouTube clips, industry resources, trade and professional association links, or research from trusted institutions that your prospects would recognize and respect.

They might include links to articles, videos, checklists, presentation decks, blog posts, frameworks, models, surveys, tools, lists, infographics, and so forth.

Whatever you choose, they need to be helpful, useful resources, directly relevant to your topic expertise and the problems your prospect told you are important to them.

You're providing a value-added touchpoint for connection so that your prospect feels they're being well served by you, even during the sales process and even before any money changes hands.

You won't get to deliver your post-sale value if your pre-sale value to your prospect is zero!

57 VALUE-DRIVEN FOLLOW-UP

How do most salespeople follow up after a first conversation?

- *Just called to touch base.*
- *I'm emailing you to check in.*
- *Wanted to circle back with you from last week.*

Those are **waste of time phrases** that have zero value for prospects. This is usually the moment they decide to go dark and disappear on you.

Because what they're hearing is:

- *Are you ready to pay me yet?*
- *Is my check ready?*
- *Yo, I could use the money now, if you don't mind.*
- *Can we run your credit card now? That just works better for me.*

ALWAYS supercharge your follow-up with additional insights, advice, or something of relevant, tangible value to your prospect.

Doesn't sound like rocket science, because it's not.

How do you add insights, advice, or tangible value?

Send them:

- Specific advice based on what they told you on previous calls
- Specific insights for their exact situation, industry, profession
- Specific resources to help them, even if they don't buy

Imagine if a professional services seller followed up with YOU with any of these messages:

Hey, by the way, I was thinking more about your situation. What might move the needle for you is X, Y, and Z. On our next call [already scheduled because you never leave one call without booking the next call!]*, I'll tell you more about it.*

This article is something I sent to another client this morning, and it made me think of our conversation last week. Take a look, and if you like it, feel free to share it with your team.

I subscribe to XYZ industry trends, and this just came across my inbox. Wanted to share it with you because it answers the exact questions you had last week. Give it a quick skim and let me know which of the 3 points was the biggest A-ha for you.

Would you be more positively inclined toward this kind of seller or the person who leaves voicemails and emails "just circling back"?

Yes, you always want to move prospects to a decision.

Yes, you always want the conversation advancing toward the sale.

The shortcut?

Add value, insights, and resources at every follow-up touch-point.

58 4 WAYS TO CREATE FOLLOW-UP MAGIC

1. **Always lead off with the prospect's comments from the previous call.**

Always start the next conversation with the prospect's comments, insights, wants, and needs from the previous call.

Make what you're saying immediately relevant to what they said they wanted, what they said they needed, what they said they're looking to solve.

This creates continuity from call to call. And it makes prospects feel heard because you remembered details that were important to them.

Hey, Jen, the last time we talked you told me you wanted X, Y, and Z. I have a few more ideas for you. And I've got a recent client win to share with you where they wanted the exact same thing.

You're connecting what they told you with another compelling reason to work with you, you're offering help and ideas, and you're advancing the sale toward the close.

2. **Ask a follow-up question to every statement they make.**

Never take a surface answer at face value.

Dig, probe, agitate, question, challenge what you're hearing. You're looking for the symptom behind the symptom and the problem behind the problem.

And in the process, each follow-up conversation becomes more valuable and enlightening to your prospect.

Your follow-up should uncover more pains, problems, challenges, and gaps, or at least remind them of what results you're helping to produce or problems you're helping them solve so they never lose sight of the big picture of why they're buying from you.

3. It's not a need or a pain until you hear it from them.

Mind reading
Assuming
Guessing
These are easy follow-up sales traps to fall into, especially if you've worked with hundreds of clients and you've seen all the same problems over and over again.

Never assume this prospect was just like your last prospect or that your next prospect will be like your current prospect.

- Never assume the issues are the same
- Never assume the wants are the same
- Never assume the needs are the same
- Never assume the fears are the same
- Never put words in their mouth

It's easy to assume and take the prospect in front of you for granted. When you do that, you are at risk for failure to listen.

Failure to listen often leads to failure to sell.

Prospects will teach you how to follow up with them if you let them.

- You have to use **their problems**
- You have to use **their issues**
- You have to use **their urgencies**
- You have to use **their goals**
- You have to use **their aspirations**
- You have to use **their desired results**

And you have to use **their language** to describe each of the above.

Whatever is important to them is important to your follow-up conversation.

Tie the follow-up right back to what they told you they want.

4. **Never leave one call without booking the next call on THEIR calendar.**

This is a key tactical step. Don't forget:

Are you in front of your calendar right now? Yes. Fantastic. Why don't we plan to talk again on Wednesday, the 14th. I've got 2:00 p.m. or 5:00 p.m. Which one do you like?

If you leave it open-ended, too many sales will get away from you.

Your prospects are lazy, busy, and befuddled.

Don't let them wander off a call and get sucked back into the daily tsunami of their work, never to be heard from again.

To download a companion resource on this topic and grab ALL your free *Do It! Selling* templates, tools, and training videos, go to: **www.doitmarketing.com/selling**

17

The Psychology of High Fees

59 YOUR MONEY AUTOBIOGRAPHY

Bad news: You have money issues.

Everyone does.

It's just a question of how aware you are of them and how much it's undermining your sales process and specifically, the way you handle the fees, money, price, and investment part of every single sales conversation.

Think that's worth looking under the hood and seeing if we can fix it?

Yup. I agree with you!

The root cause of our money issues is that every single aspect of our society, from parents to teachers to the media, is filled with negative money messages about why money, wealth, or being rich is filthy, corrupt, and disgusting.

How many times have you heard:

- It's not polite to talk about money
- Money doesn't grow on trees
- Money is dirty
- Money is the root of all evil
- Money can't buy happiness
- Money isn't everything
- There are more important things than money
- Rich people are greedy and selfish

Look at the way the super-rich are consistently portrayed in TV shows and movies. Hedge fund managers, corporate CEOs, attorneys, consultants, or investors are all horrible, evil, terrible people.

No wonder that screwy money beliefs are a big sales obstacle, so much so that **your internal judgments and beliefs about money** might be your main roadblock to making more, better, and bigger sales happen.

Money is often a taboo subject, more "forbidden" than sex in our culture.

Answer the following questions to begin working on getting "unstuck" about the role of money in your life.

1. What do you think about money? [The first answer that comes to you is perfect!]

2. What's your attitude toward managing money? Do you avoid it? Obsess about it?

3. My bank account is:

4. Discussing money makes me feel:

_____

_____

5. Money always:

_____

_____

6. For me to make more money, I must:

_____

_____

7. If I make too much money, then:

_____

_____

8. I can't make a lot of money, because:

_____

_____

9. I deserve to earn:

_____

_____

Once you've answered these questions, write a "money auto-biography," which is simply a truthful account of significant life events from the perspective of money.

These questions might start you thinking:

1. When do you first recall having money of your own?
2. How free were you to decide what to do with that money?
3. How was money discussed in your family?
4. Can you think of a concrete image that illustrates the role money has in your life?
5. Have you ever seen money used in a way that hurts other people?
6. When you face money decisions, how do you feel? Challenged? Elated? Anxious?
7. What is the most difficult experience you've had in which money played a part, either openly or covertly?

To download this exercise in electronic form and grab all your free *Do It! Selling* templates, tools, and training videos, go to **www.doitmarketing.com/selling**

60 TEST-DRIVE BEING RICH

Imagine charging your clients more money than you've ever charged before.

Think $500,000 consulting contracts and $150,000 coaching agreements and $45,000 keynote speaking fees.

I can hear you now: "Newman, are you nuts? I've never sold anything even close to that!"

That resistance is a real sales problem if you want to elevate your business into the world of high-value, high-fee clients.

Breaking through that resistance requires nothing more and nothing less than changing your money mindset, which will have an enormous impact on your ability to close much bigger deals for much higher fees.

Perhaps when you see fees like $500,000 or $150,000 or $45,000 your immediate knee-jerk response is, "I could never charge that much."

I love when my clients ask me for pricing advice on a particular project and, when I tell them what to charge, they respond with that phrase.

It's a huge learning moment.

When you think about it, it actually does not make any logical sense.

Of course you can charge "that much." It's a free country, and you can charge whatever you want.

What my client is REALLY saying is "I would never pay that much. That is beyond my realm of possibility of what somebody would pay for my program, my consulting, my coaching, my expertise, my professional services."

The good news is that YOU have nothing to do with your pricing.

Let me repeat: YOU have nothing to do with your pricing.

Why?

Because what is a lot of money to you is NOT a lot of money to others.

- You may live in a $500,000 house, and your client lives in a $5 million house
- You may drive a $30,000 car, and your client drives a $120,000 car
- You may wear a Timex, and your client may wear a Rolex

You get the idea.

You are not your clients.

You're about to make this insight viscerally real for yourself.

Here's your mission, should you choose to accept it:

You're going to test-drive being rich.

I want you to go out and shop for a high-end luxury item, something that is meaningful to you: a fun toy or a bucket list item, a dream object that gets you really excited.

For some people, it's cars. Go test-drive a Maserati or BMW or Tesla.

For some people, it's boats. For some people, it's high-end furniture. For some people, it's fancy shoes, fancy clothing, fancy watches, fancy jewelry.

Whatever it is, take yourself out for a shopping experience, either in person or online.

Look at prices and make phone calls, especially if you see a piece of jewelry and it's marked "price by request."

Be the person who requests!

Hi. I'm on your website. I'm looking at the diamond-encrusted bracelets. I see this one over here from Harry Winston. It says price by request. I'm curious: How much is that piece?

And then let them tell you it's $125,000. If you're in the store, don't just look; try it on.

Check out the cockpit of that boat that is $280,000. Hear those twin engines rumbling in the water.

Find out what the inside of that $90,000 Tesla smells like. How do the seats feel? How do you like that "space shuttle" acceleration when your foot presses down on the pedal? (Can't say gas pedal, because it's a Tesla!)

One of my clients took this exercise to heart. She test-drove a blue Tesla, a car she's had her eye on for some time but thought it was too much of a luxury.

She completed the test-drive.

But she did not leave the dealership.

She bought the car!

The idea here is to put yourself in a position to experience something you might not otherwise buy. Something "too expensive, too fancy, too high-end, too luxury."

The two lessons for you:

The first lesson is that there is no such thing as "too expensive, too fancy, too high-end, too luxury." It's all relative.

What's expensive to you is not expensive to others.

The second lesson: When you're browsing at the high-end jeweler, when you're walking around the BMW dealership, when you're trying something on in that designer boutique, please notice that **you are NOT alone.** There are other shoppers there, and they are there to BUY, not browse. People spend big money all the time on all kinds of things that, to you, may seem "out of reach" or "too expensive."

You are not your client.

And there are clients who will invest whatever you charge for your programs and your services.

You've been looking for love (and clients) in all the wrong places.

You haven't been putting your services in front of the right buyers, and you haven't been using the right kind of outcome-based language.

Remember: no one forces somebody to buy a $125,000 diamond-encrusted Harry Winston bracelet. There are no sales tactics required. There are no gimmicks. There's no trickery. There's no manipulation.

People buy a $125,000 piece of jewelry because they want a $125,000 piece of jewelry.

High fees are not about persuasion. They're about value and desire.

61 INCONCEIVABLE!

"You keep using that word. I do not think it means what you think it means."

—Inigo Montoya, *The Princess Bride*

The word *GOAL* is one of the most misunderstood words in entrepreneurship.

Smart goals are stupid.

You've heard that old cliché, right? SMART goals is an acronym for:

- Specific
- Measurable
- Achievable
- Realistic
- Time-bound

Except two-fifths of that formula is garbage: **achievable** and **realistic** are the two problem areas and they keep many smart, ambitious salespeople stuck in mediocrity.

Truth is, hitting BIG sales goals doesn't happen by accident.

The problem with traditional goal setting is that you tend to set goals based not on what you really want but on what you think you're going to get.

Bad news: You don't really have goals. You have expectations.

Even worse, you may think **setting** big goals is the secret.

In reality, HITTING big goals is the secret! You need to be fully committed to doing so; otherwise, even big goals become pipe dreams that actually demotivate you!

It's not about CAN-do or WANT-to-do.

It's about WILL-do, with no excuses.

Let's say it's November 30, and I ask you, *How much revenue do you really, really, really want by the end of December?*

You might say, *Well, it's December. It's the holidays, I'm busy, I have to wash the dog, buy Hannukah gifts, I'm just starting to read* Do It! Selling, *so my sales skills aren't where they need to be. You know, boy, I could realistically close $10,000 this month.*

That wasn't my question.

You answered, *I could realistically close $10,000 this month.*

I didn't ask what you could do; I asked what you WANTED.

In other words, I asked you for a goal, and you responded with an expectation. And a rather low expectation at that.

Here's a different type of response. See if you can FEEL the difference:

Well, David, my sales plan and revenue target is based on $30,000 a month, or $360,000 for the year. The answer is easy: Between now and the end of December, I will earn $30,000.

That's it. That's a will-do sales goal.

Rain or shine, happy or sad, Christmas, Kwanzaa, Father's Day, Labor Day, or Saint Patrick's Day. No stories. No excuses. No BS.

What do you really and truly WANT?

Ask yourself: Are you setting goals or just listing expectations?

62 YOUR HIGH-FEE LIST OF MYTHS

Strap in and hang on! You're getting my "High-Fee List O'Myths" about all the reasons consultants, coaches, and experts like you give for NOT embracing the high-fee expert model.

Some of these reasons are plain dumb, and some are devilishly logical because they sound like they make perfect sense, but they're completely wrong anyway.

Here we go:

Myth #1: "My clients can't afford higher fees."

Truth #1: You need better clients. Stop selling to broke-ass losers, and everything in your business will improve: your marketing, sales, finance, operations, and customer service.

Myth #2: "If I suddenly start charging way higher fees, I'll price myself out of the market, and no one will buy from me."

Truth #2: If you start charging way higher fees, you will TURN OFF the "freeple," the people who want everything free but never buy anyway; you will REPEL the "cheaple," the bottom-feeding morons who want everything cheap and are the biggest pain in the ass when they do buy; and you'll (finally) ATTRACT your people.

Food for thought: Have you ever considered what it would mean to your business to dramatically raise your fees and suddenly price yourself INTO a whole new (higher) level of client?

Myth #3: "I need to generate cash flow right now, so I'll keep selling my next few clients or projects at the old prices, or offer discounts to get even quicker sales."

Truth #3: Low fees have nothing to do with quicker sales. And high fees have nothing to do with slower sales. This is total nonsense. In fact, it is the opposite in many cases: Your low-fee clients take forever to decide to buy. And your high-fee clients buy on the spot when they see the right offer expressed in the right way to solve their exact problems at the right (premium) fee.

Food for thought: Your professional services are not commodities like we studied in 11th grade economics, and there is NO connection between supply and demand when it comes to pricing. Lowering your fees will NOT get you more clients. Raising your fees will NOT get you fewer clients. You're not a pork belly. This is all about connecting with DIFFERENT, better, smarter clients.

Myth #4: "All things being equal, everyone wants to pay less for my services, and I'm having enough trouble closing sales at my old prices!"

Truth #4: All things are never equal. Your experience may be limited to the people who are attracted to your low prices. If you do a customer survey at Walmart, very few of those people will own a Porsche.

Does that mean there's no market for Porsches? Interestingly, Porsche makes $23,000 net profit on every car it sells, making it one of the most profitable auto brands.

Myth #5: "People buy based on price. To sell more, I should probably cut my prices, not raise them!"

Truth #5: People buy who they are. There are Timex people. And there are Rolex people.

A Timex prospect would never pay more than $150 for a watch (the average cost of a Timex is around $40). That's just who they are.

A Rolex prospect would never pay LESS than $2,500 for a watch (the average cost of a Rolex is around $12,000). That's just who they are.

People buy based on their IDENTITY. Think about this: There are Mac people and PC people. There are BMW drivers, and there are Ferrari drivers. There are Walmart shoppers, and there are Target shoppers. Almost zero crossover.

Stop selling to Timex and start selling to Rolex, and you'll discover that premium clients EXPECT to pay premium fees. Anything less, and they say, "Hmmmm, this doesn't sound like it's for me."

Boom! That was the sound of your low-fee business model, your low-fee excuses, and your low-fee services getting blown to smithereens.

63 FEES ARE YOUR FILTER

The more you charge, the better clients you will attract because your fees are a filter for the clients that you most want to work with.

When you charge too little, you attract the entirely wrong layer of the marketplace.

These are the tire kickers, price shoppers, goofballs, and goobers who do everything on the cheap, need to be chased and cajoled, and who will nickel-and-dime you even if they end up buying, which they rarely do.

Wouldn't you prefer to escape the price-driven sale?

Do you want to serve the top of your market with premium positioning and premium fees?

You do! You do!!

But something might be holding you back: the fear that your prospects won't be able to afford your premium fees.

And you may be right.

In which case, as I said before, you need to work on **finding better prospects.**

But when you talk to the right prospect in the right way using the right language for the right reasons, and they can instantly see how your services can help them solve a major problem or achieve a major result, they almost always *find the money*. They will *reallocate the budget*. They will bend over backward to work with you because now they see the value.

Don't guess or assume who can and can't afford your fees.

64 EASY=PRICELESS

One last psychological obstacle we need to break through for you.

It's the problem of EASY.

As a trusted advisor, consultant, or professional expert, you probably enjoy the work of your work much more than you enjoy selling.

You love your work. You love your clients. On your best days, I bet you even think to yourself, *This is so cool. I can't believe they're paying me for this. I'm having so much fun!*

The work is perfectly suited to your skills, background, experience, and interests.

Because of that, you find the work easy.

Engaging. Energizing. Effortless.

And it's true: When you operate in your zone of genius, you're in a state of flow. Things come easily to you.

DANGER: When your work seems easy, you undervalue it like crazy.

Truth bomb: You will always make the most money and have the most impact delivering work that comes easily to you but is difficult for others.

So please, just because it's easy, just because you love it, just because you would do it for free does not mean it does not have serious economic value in the marketplace.

In fact, the opposite is true.

When you deploy your hard-earned skills, passions, abilities, and aptitude to help a client solve a problem or achieve an outcome, the BEST person for the job, and the person who will deliver the greatest value, is the person for whom it is easy, effortless, and fun.

Ancient Zen wisdom: "A master at work is a master at play."

18

High-Fee Sales

65 THE INESCAPABLE REALITY OF YOUR REVENUES

Remember 3rd grade?

Your teacher gave you word problems like, "You're selling apples for 50 cents each. Grace wants to buy 3 apples. How much does Grace owe you?"

Back then, you learned the formula:

PRICE x QUANTITY = TOTAL.

That's the same formula for what I call *the inescapable reality of your revenues*. There's no way around it.

Let's say your sales target is $125K per year.

Any number you choose can't be floating untethered in outer space as a vague generality. It needs you to answer a few simple questions about how you'll hit $125K:

- Doing what?
- For whom?
- At what price point?
- How many times a month?

Maybe your target is $250K. Same set of questions.

Doing what? For whom? At what price point? How many?

Want to hit $500K per year? Same questions.

Let's use $300K as a nice healthy sales target as we discuss different ways to approach the Price x Quantity = Total formula.

There are many kinds of $300K businesses.

You can sell 300 things for $1,000 and have a $300,000 business.

Or you can sell 10 things for $30,000.

Selling 10 things for $30K is very different than selling 300 things for $1K. At the end of the year, those are both $300K businesses, but they're different from a lead generation, prospecting, inviting, and conversing standpoint.

For professional services sellers like you and me, I'm a big believer in high fees and low volume.

A typical high-fee consultant, coach, or expert doesn't need hundreds of clients per year.

I'll bet if you sell 5, 10, or 12 things for between $20,000 and $150,000 per year, you would be super happy. That's the key to a multiple 6-figure or even 7-figure professional services firm. From there, you can start to scale even faster if you want to.

Do the math! Feel the power!!

66 THE PRICE IS RIGHT

What's the secret that helps high-fee experts land high-dollar deals that may seem ridiculous to you right now?

Deals that might be worth $93,000 or $170,000 or $250,000 when you may be more accustomed to selling the same or similar things for one-tenth of those amounts?

The secret is context.

Specifically...

The context of value and the contrast of scale.

During your sales conversations, you will be probing for budget, presenting some fee ranges, and talking money.

Before that happens, you want to set the context for the value they'll get from you and your work.

Here's why:

Any price without context is a price that's too high.

Imagine a salesperson comes up to you and says:

I have this fantastic service to sell you. It's $250,000.

What's your immediate reaction likely to be?

"I don't think so. 250 grand is a lot of money. No thanks!"

Now imagine that same salesperson comes up to you and says:

We're going to solve your $7 million problem, and the investment is just $250,000.

Now you're thinking, "This is the bargain of the decade! I am so IN!"

How do you put your price into context?

To establish context, quantify the value of fixing the client's problem.

In the example above, I said, "We're going to solve a $7 million problem for you."

This context comes from questioning your prospect. Never assume or use theoretical numbers.

Always ask prospects for their numbers. Ask about their people, profits, processes, dollars, hours, percentages, whatever makes sense in light of what you're selling.

For example, where did that $7 million dollar problem come from?

It came from the following set of questions and answers:

Salesperson: *What's the average deal that your reps are selling at these trade shows?*
Prospect: *Well, that's the thing. They're not selling ANY-THING at the trade shows.*
Salesperson: *What were you expecting trade show sales to be last year?*
Prospect: *Usually, we walk away with 5 to 7 deals at each show.*
Salesperson: *How much is an average deal worth?*
Prospect: *You mean for a wholesaler or a distributor?*
Salesperson: *Give me both.*
Prospect: *For a wholesaler, it's usually $100K, and for a distributor it could be twice that.*
Salesperson: *Wow! Average of $150K times 5? So you're saying it's $750K of trade show sales that are not coming in? Did I get that math right?*
Prospect: *Yep.*

Salesperson: *Hoo boy...and how many shows do your reps attend each year?*

Prospect: *Ten.*

Salesperson: *So you're saying you're short 10 times $750K, or $7.5 million, of sales that could be coming from those trade shows if the reps knew how to talk to customers more persuasively?*

Prospect: *You got it. Ugh, it's even more depressing when you do the math like that.*

Salesperson: *And that's purely trade shows. Your reps also sell other ways, correct? Outbound calls, online demos, and referrals, yes?*

Prospect: *Yes. We are leaving SO much money on the table, now that you mention these other opportunities...*

Salesperson: *I almost hate to ask, but how many other $7.5 million problems do you think the team has?*

Prospect: *Trust me. A lot.*

Salesperson: *Are you willing to make the investment to solve these problems once and for all?*

Prospect: *Yes. And the sooner, the better. When can you start?*

This is where you get to deliver the magic words we talked about at the beginning of this story:

I have great news. We're going to solve your $7 million problem, and the investment is just $250,000.

Presenting that $7 million figure shifts the whole conversation.

Your $250,000 price tag just shrank into a small, reasonable figure.

That's the contrast of scale.

We went from "250 grand is a lot of money" all the way to $250K to solve a $7-million problem?

"When can you start?"

Remember: The prospect MUST believe that they do, in fact, have a $7 million problem.

They will only see the contrast of scale if you helped them to come up with their own numbers themselves!

No guessing, no putting words in their mouth, no theory. Just using their own hard numbers that they provide as they answer your simple questions around their urgent problems.

Always use numbers your prospects give you.

Why? Because...

Prospects never argue with their own data.

Here's a different example to give you more practice.

Let's say you have a leadership development program that you're selling to corporate clients.

You have a prospect who's already expressed interest. They know they have a problem, and they have the need, the desire, and the urgency to solve it.

Start off by getting two key numbers from the client.

Question 1: *How many leaders are you thinking of putting through this program?*

The client responds, "About 20."

Question 2: *I'm curious, are they frontline managers, senior executives, somewhere in the middle? And for level-setting purposes, what's the average salary of these leaders?*

Tip: When you ask the second question, throw out a number and lowball it. "What is it, around $60,000, $70,000?"

When you lowball the number, the prospect will respond with something like, "No, not $60,000. These are upper-middle managers! They make between $100,000 to $120,000. They're on the VP career path."

Now it's time to do some math.

If you're not a math whiz, take out your phone and fire up the old calculator app.

Punch in 20 times $100,000, and you get $2 million.

Then you reply to your prospect, "What we're really talking about is moving the needle on the performance of about $2 million of payroll value. Is that right?"

Don't just present the number. Ask, confirm, and get them to repeat it.

"Yeah, that's about right. I never thought of it that way, but you're in the ballpark."

Now for the final step.

They are going to use their numbers to calculate their fabulous return on investment for your services. Here's what to say to make that happen.

"Let's be superconservative here. Let's say we made these 20 managers just 10 percent more effective. We usually hit 20 percent, 30 percent, or higher, but I want to be conservative here. Ten percent of $2 million is what?"

Don't do the math for them.

When they do the math, they tell you that 10 percent of $2 million is $200,000. Now you can use that number because it is *their number*.

"So if we work on these 20 leaders for the next 90 days, and we make them just 10 percent more effective, which again is very low in my experience, $200,000 falls right to the bottom line. Is that about right?"

Always ask that confirming question based on their math and their numbers.

They've just told you that your program will save them $200,000. What a deal! As the recap below shows, that's a 10x ROI.

- Salary value of 20 execs = **$2 million**
- Making managers **10 percent more effective** = 10 percent x salary value (saved time, saved money, reduced turnover, increased performance) = **$200,000**
- Cost of your program = **$20,000**
- Return on Investment = $200,000/$20,000 = **10x ROI**

The moment you present your fee or fee range, you will have established the context of value and the contrast of scale.

Try not to look surprised when the next thing you hear is, "When can you start?"

67 AND WHO ELSE?

No buyer buys in a vacuum.

Nobody spends $50 for no reason.

At the same time, buyers will gladly spend $50,000 to solve a $1 million problem.

The questions below will help your buyer expand the **context of value** and the **contrast of scale** around hiring you to help them either a) solve a problem, b) create an outcome, or c) both.

Who else will notice if we fix this?

What information does this typically uncover?

You'll find out who else is impacted by solving this problem or overcoming this obstacle. You may discover additional decision-makers you want to meet in the company. You may find other stakeholders who can either help or hinder the sale.

The answer may also reveal other opportunities in the company for your services. Or even hint at potential internal and external referral sources.

My CEO is looking to me to fix this problem. Our CFO is very concerned about this. And the head of international operations too. That's why I'm talking to you.

Will that be a big deal to them? How so?

You want a "yes." And then you want to probe and find out in as much detail as possible WHY this is a big deal, what are the consequences, what will they gain if they fix it, what will they lose if they don't?

Whose butt is on the line, and how hot is the fire under their chair?

This is an answer you want to establish early on because it prevents the "bad timing" objection or the "we're so busy" objection or even the price objection.

Bust these objections in advance, take them out of play, and make sure your witness hears themselves say these things out loud, just like a good courtroom attorney.

And who else?

"And who else" is going to be your upselling, cross-selling, deal-expanding question.

There is no bad time to ask this question.

For example:

- Who will be invited to this training? **And who else?**
- Who is going to get this coaching? **And who else?**
- Who will be in the audience for this speech? **And who else?**
- Who is involved in that process? **And who else?**
- Who needs to sign off on this? **And who else?**
- Who will be impacted if this fails? **And who else?**
- Who's going to look like a hero if it works? **And who else?**
- Whose budget might this affect? **And who else?**
- Which executives will want this in their division? **And who else?**
- Which regional heads should we invite? **And who else?**
- Who might we want to get input from? **And who else?**

What do you think the bottom-line impact will be in terms of dollars?

Everything either makes money or costs money.

There are the four obvious sources of ROI, such as:

- Make money
- Save money
- Make time
- Save time

But everything has a dollars-and-cents impact. Even seemingly intangible things, like:

- Employee retention
- Recruiting
- Morale
- Corporate culture
- Diversity
- Employee engagement
- Productivity
- Performance
- Efficiency

- Effectiveness
- Collaboration
- Innovation
- Teamwork
- Leadership
- Communications
- Customer Service
- Strategy

...and pretty much any other problem you're hired to fix or results you're hired to create.

Even if YOU don't know the dollars-and-cents value, sometimes your prospect will. And if they don't, often you can help them think it through.

Does that come out of your budget? Who ends up feeling that loss? Does that affect profitability? Does that affect salaries or bonuses?

Notice we're not saying YOUR salary or bonus, but that's how they're going to take it.

It totally impacts my bonus. And in fact, it impacts our whole team because I need to hire four new positions. Right now, I can't. And I really need those four people.

You probably have a few competing priorities besides fixing this. What are they?

This question leads to another mother lode of information.

You will get a sense of your prospect's urgency, how this project fits into their other priorities, and what might be an obstacle or distraction that prevents the sale.

You'll also get answers that might help you expand the scope and scale of the deal.

For example, if you're discussing a team-building initiative, your prospect may tell you about competing initiatives around corporate culture and leadership development.

Well, that's interesting. I don't really see that as competing at all. In fact, we help many of our clients in all three of those areas: team building, culture, and leadership. You don't want 3 cooks in the kitchen. If you're like our other large clients in the middle of a merger, you probably want an integrated, unified approach to solving all three of these problems. Can we talk about what that might look like?

What you thought was a $30,000 deal just became a $90,000 deal.

68 17 GREAT ANSWERS TO "HOW MUCH DO YOU CHARGE?"

For professional services sellers, the #1 deal-killer question is, "How much do you charge?"

Especially when it's asked too early, out of context, and before you've established any sort of relationship with the prospect or any sort of value for the project.

In short, if you blow the answer, your prospect is gone.

Here are three things **NOT** to do:

1. Quote a random price out of thin air (unless you sell hair-cuts for $18 or oil changes for $34.95 or you do book-keeping for $65/hr)
2. Act surprised or unprepared for the question ("Uhhh... what do you mean?")
3. Get defensive or go on a rant about how "all people care about these days is price, price, price."

Some of the answers you're about to get are evergreen, some you can adapt to your own personality, and some you may want to keep in reserve until just the right moment with just the right prospect.

Here we go...

"How much do you charge?"

1. A lot. Why do you ask?
2. I don't think we're there yet because I don't know what you're buying.

3. I'll answer your question in a moment, but to give you a more accurate answer, may I ask you three questions first?

4. Well, the friends and family rate might apply, but we're not friends yet. Do you mind if I ask you a few friendly questions that will help us answer your pricing question together?

5. It's $9 million until I know what you're buying. Can we spend a few minutes narrowing that down to help you lower the price?

6. I have good news, and I have bad news. The good news is that you don't have a $500,000 problem. The bad news is that you don't have a $10,000 problem either. If you can help me answer some key questions, we'll both know a lot more about what your investment might look like.

7. If it works, it's cheap. If it doesn't, it's expensive.

8. Let's talk about what you're trying to accomplish first, and then we'll work out some pricing options based on that.

9. Do you want the Ferrari version, the Lexus version, or the VW Bug?

10. A project like the one you're asking about ranges from $X to $Y. Sometimes a little more. Not usually less. Is that what you were expecting to invest?

11. There's no good answer to that question in a vacuum. Can we talk a little more about what you're hoping we can do for you? Then I'll give you some pricing options that make sense for your budget.

12. A project of this scope only makes sense if it's already in your budget. Nobody wakes up one day and suddenly finds the money to solve these kinds of problems. If you can share the budget range you have set aside for this, I can tell you if it makes sense for us to talk any further.

13. I have a feeling that if I quote a random number right now, I'll be dead in the water. Do you mind if I ask you some questions to get a better idea of what your goals are? Then the numbers we talk about will be specific to you and your situation.

14. Just like you need to make an educated decision about which partner or resource to hire, I need to give you an educated answer to your pricing question. And I'm feeling pretty dumb right now, since we just started talking. Mind if we have a 10-minute conversation about your situation? After that, I'll have a much better idea of what you're after and some different ways we can help.

15. Sounds like price is the most important factor to you. In my experience, everything is expensive until you want it. Can we talk about what you want and then work our way to the pricing options based on that?

16. It's more than a cab ride to [local landmark e.g., the Empire State Building] but less than [the landmark e.g., the building]. If we can chat for 10 minutes about why you called, I can give you a much more specific answer. Do you have 10 minutes now, or shall we look at our calendars?

17. Until I have a better idea of what you want, and whether or not we can even help, any number I give you is going to be too high. Would it be all right if we spend a few minutes discussing why you called? Then if we can help, I'll get you the pricing options you need. And if we can't, I'll refer you to some other great resources that do things we don't. Fair enough?

69 ALWAYS END ON POSSIBILITY, NOT AFFORDABILITY

Never end a sales conversation on the topic of pricing, money, or fees.

"Well, it's $25,000. And I sure hope you have that $25,000 in the budget. Bye!"

Not exactly an inspiring way to close a sales conversation.

You want to end your sales conversations on a note of possibility, not affordability.

Remind them why they're doing this.

Restate the reasons they told you were important to them.

Reinforce the value, impact, results, outcomes, and the emotional payoff of solving those problems and achieving those outcomes.

Here's the magic trick:

Reframe the fee conversation inside the value conversation.

I have great news! Based on everything you just told me, this project we'll do together to solve problem X for your team, create outcome Y for you personally, and generate result Z for the whole company is probably less than you think. We can get this done for between $25K–$45K, depending how fast you'd like to go. And you'll never have to worry about symptom A, that B problem you mentioned will be ancient history, and outcome C will become your new normal before you know it. Let me sharpen my pencil and get back to you with some specific options. How does that sound?

Remind them of their key strategic initiative, their big company-wide goals, those huge problems that were making them nuts, and that big project their CEO is betting the company on. Always end on possibility, not affordability.

19

Closing Time

70 CRAZY SCARY BAD: CLOSING QUESTIONS

This is the part of the horror movie where the axe murderer finally breaks through the door, everyone screams, blood is splattering everywhere, and the screen fades to black.

What am I talking about?

Everyone's favorite sales nightmare: "closing" questions.

Relax, Freddy Krueger. It's not that bad.

(FYI, Freddy's weapon of choice wasn't an axe. It was a bladed glove. So c'mon!)

Done the right way, these are not scary questions.

Not scary for sellers and not scary for buyers.

Imagine you're out to dinner with someone special, and you just finished a beautiful seven-course meal at a gourmet restaurant. We're talking white linen tablecloth, 3 kinds of forks, 2 wineglasses, the full deal.

Then your waiter comes up to the two of you and politely asks, "Would you like coffee? Would you like dessert?"

Chances are small that you would stand up, throw down your fork, get enraged, and yell at the waiter, *How dare you ask me that question. We're having this beautiful meal. And now you have the gall to ask if we would like coffee or dessert?! What is wrong with you? This is outrageous! Honey, let's get out of here!*

Why are these closing questions not likely to upset you?

Because they're a natural, organic extension of everything that has come before.

They're easy, natural, logical questions that most diners expect to answer.

Some will want coffee and dessert.

Some will want one but not the other.

And some will decline both.

All those answers are good answers.

Now, because you're not a waiter in a fancy restaurant, and frankly I'm not even sure why they give you 3 forks in those places, here are some real closing questions for you:

Key closing question #1: Does this sound like something you want to do?

After a deep-dive diagnostic sales conversation (the great meal), it would make perfect sense to ask your prospect:

Does this sound like something you want to do?

Other variations and formats for your closing questions:

- Based on what we talked about, what would you like to do next?
- Would you like to get started?
- Does this sound like something that makes sense for you right now?
- How would you like us to proceed?
- When might you like to get this underway?
- Is there any reason you would not want to move ahead?
- How about we work together to make this happen?
- Let's work on this together. What do you think?
- Would you like our help to implement the plan we just talked about?
- We have several good options here. Which one sounds best to you?
- Based on everything you said, it's a green light from me. Is it a green light from you?

All these variations work because they are just a natural extension of the sales conversation you've been having.

Key closing question #2: What credit card would you like to put that on?

This is my favorite question. The moment they agree that they're IN, we need to strike while the iron is hot.

Use this 2-part variation for corporate clients:

- Shall I send you an invoice or do you use a purchase order process of some kind?
- If I get the invoice over to you in the next few minutes, is there any reason we couldn't get that check processed by the end of tomorrow?

You don't want your invoice sitting on your new client's printer for 4 days; or worse, sitting in some accounts payable bin in their accounting department for 4 months. Been there, done that.

When you directly ask a great client to expedite the process, they usually will.

Remember our dual mantras from the "Now, Now, Now" chapter?

Time kills deals. Money loves speed.

For both those reasons, please do not delay, do not send links, do not trust that the client will process payment, give you a deposit, or otherwise do anything if they don't do it right then or within 24 hours.

When you ask, "What credit card would you like to put that on?" you take that credit card information right there in the moment.

By the way, I've seen large company executives process $70,000 payments using corporate American Express cards.

Platinum cards (and higher) have no limit. Don't assume that the credit card question is only relevant when selling to individuals or small business owners.

Ask and ye shall receive.

When you expect (and ask for) payment NOW, you get paid much more quickly.

71 NEGOTIATE, DON'T CAVE

Let's define these two terms:

Caving on price is lowering your fee for no reason.

Negotiating on price is taking value off the table.

Never lower your fees without taking commensurate value off the table.

If a prospect asks you to lower the price, ask them:

What would you like me to leave out of what we discussed?

Typically, they don't want to leave out anything. They just want you to drop your price.

Firmly and kindly give them several options:

- You can **leave out elements** of your consulting, training, speaking, or coaching program that you normally include
- You can reduce the amount of **depth, duration, and detail** that you were going to deliver (including reducing quantity, frequency, or capacity)
- You can **deliver "off the shelf" services** with no customization, no tailoring, and no personalization of any kind
- You can **remove prework** (research, assessments, surveys, interviews) or **remove follow-up work** (post-assessments, aftercare, check-ins, tune-ups, ongoing access to you for support)

Don't be surprised when you stick to your integrity and your buyer sees you're not willing to do the same work for less money, they'll buy the full value at the full price.

72 YOGURT PROPOSALS

If you use proposals, please keep in mind:

Proposals are like yogurt. They have an expiration date.

Always put an expiration date on proposals and make it clear and obvious.

Once on the cover page and again on the pricing page.

Do not be subtle.

The language is simple:

The terms, conditions, and pricing for this proposal expire in 14 days.

or

The terms, conditions, and pricing for this proposal expire August 11.

Expiration dates mean deadlines, and deadlines mean decisions.

An expiration date gives you an organic reason to follow up.

Hey, Bob, it's August 7. The proposal I sent has an August 11 expiration date. I know we're talking tomorrow at 1:30 Pacific, but I just wanted to make sure everything looks good on your end. And here's another idea/another resource/another [cool thing] for you. Talk to you tomorrow.

For timing your expiration dates, I recommend 7 to 14 days out, not longer.

If you want faster sales and shorter sales cycles, EXPECT faster sales and shorter sales cycles.

The best way to expect shorter sales cycles is to ENFORCE them.

73 THE FEE-PAID PILOT

Sometimes, when a professional services deal is at the tipping point, when it's almost a "yes," you can close the deal with a fee-paid pilot.

Think about the word *pilot* as it's used in the television industry.

The network will order a pilot episode of a new show, and if the pilot tests well, they order the first season of episodes for a new series.

The word *pilot* implies if they like what they see, there's a lot more to come.

Of course, if they don't love it, all bets are off.

Everyone goes home. You tear up the contracts. Series canceled.

A fee-paid pilot is a one-time experience. Once the pilot is delivered, the client needs to decide: buy the full program or terminate the relationship.

You might have noticed I'm NOT recommending the notion of a **free** pilot.

Free is too easy to ignore and too easy to say yes to without any real commitment.

Too many times the "hot" prospect takes the free pilot, then runs.

Turns out they were hot for free. But they were not so hot to pay you what you're worth.

Forget the free pilot.

Another piece of advice: don't be tempted to **discount** the pilot.

If one consulting day with you is $10,000, and your fee-paid pilot is a one-day strategic whiteboard session, then the investment is $10,000.

Some prospects might argue that since they will be buying a $250,000 engagement if they're happy with the pilot, they should get a discount on the pilot.

The quick-and-easy answer is, "Nope."

Simply mention that if they love what's happening and decide to hire you after your fee-paid pilot, you'll credit the pilot fee toward the follow-on project.

There is one other feasible option: the **fee-waived** pilot.

The fee-waived pilot is a half-day executive work session with decision-makers only.

This is very important. You're not doing this for HR or the training group; you're doing this for the **high-level executives ONLY.**

Structure this session as an investigative in-person sales call.

The output of that half day: a detailed diagnosis of their current situation and a detailed prescription plan for the work they should do with you in the proper order and with timelines for implementation.

While you technically are "waiving" your fee for this half-day diagnostic session, **make them pay something.** They must show you that they're serious and committed.

If you travel to them in person, waive the fee but let them know that they'll prepay for your flight and hotel. If they won't cut a check for that, they are not a serious prospect.

If you do this remotely, charge a few hundred dollars as an assessment or materials fee. Again, if they're not willing to invest a few hundred dollars, you're wasting your time.

Money talks. Hot air walks.

74 NEGOTIATE UP

In sales, most professional services experts assume that the word *negotiate* means "negotiate down."

Why not negotiate up?

Think back to a time in your own experience when a prospect said, "I don't want this for that price," and they ended up buying something better for a higher price.

Why does this happen?

Because the higher-priced option gets them to the ultimate outcome they want.

Want to practice your "Negotiate Up" muscles?

The next time a prospect asks you, "Is that your best price? Can you work with me on the fees? Is that a firm number, or can we negotiate?"

Your new answer is going to be:

Absolutely. How much MORE would you like to pay?

When they start laughing, explain to them that you're serious **because you want them to solve the problem** with a solution that WORKS and LASTS, and not spend money on yet another half-baked partial effort that's doomed to fail.

Explain that half measures and baby steps and Band-Aids ARE cheaper in the short term. But what about the long term?

Imagine if you suggested to your next prospect:

Rather than cut the program, rather than do less, why don't we brainstorm for a couple of minutes on what more looks like? More effective, more comprehensive, more results, and helping more of your people on a faster timeline.

You will be surprised how many buyers will go with you on that exploration:

OK, what does more comprehensive look like? What does more results look like?

Prospects can't buy a premium option you never present.

Now that you know how to negotiate up, you'll look forward to the next time a prospect asks, "Can we negotiate?"

75 EXPECT TO WIN EVERY DEAL

It makes an ENORMOUS difference!

Will you win 100 percent of all your deals?

Of course not, but you'll win a whole heck of a lot more if you expect to win all the time.

My friend marketing and sales coach Michael Charest calls this Positive Expectation Without Attachment To the Outcome (PEWATO, for short).

PEWATO means you stay neutral, but you expect prospects to buy because it's in their best interest, and it's only logical.

Who wouldn't buy from you?

Your clients get amazing, fantastic results!

You're transforming their lives!

You're transforming their business!

You're solving their problems!

Why would anyone who's a good fit not buy?

Here's a mental nugget to spark your thinking:

Do you believe your prospects' objections?
Because I don't. And neither should you.

The moment you believe those objections, you will start to accept them, then you'll start to expect them, and then your sales results are doomed.

You must stay in what Apple cofounder Steve Jobs liked to call his "reality distortion matrix," where everything was possible with no limits on technology, time, money, or resources.

He never believed, or even acknowledged, objections, limitations, or constraints on what the rest of the world (including

Apple engineers and designers) thought was possible, doable, practical, or realistic.

In my "sales distortion matrix," every prospect who doesn't buy is truly missing out, and I feel sadness and empathy for them because of all the problems they'll continue to have, and all the breakthrough results they'll never get because they're not working with us.

If you've dug deep, probed, uncovered, and shown your prospect exactly what they could solve or achieve in their business, their career, with their money, with their family, in whatever areas you solve problems and create results...

I cannot imagine you getting on a call with a great prospect and expecting them to say anything other than "YES!" Can you?

20

That's a Wrap!

76 7 THINGS SALES PROS MUST DO DAILY

Here are the top 7 things that professional services sellers like you must do every single day:

1. **Revisit your goals, milestones, and metrics** for the day, week, month, and quarter (financial, marketing, sales, operations).

Ramifications if not done daily: You lose sight of the big picture and get pulled off your game by distractions, trivia, and grunt work.

2. **Put new prospects on your radar** via strategic high-relevance outreach.

Ramifications if not done daily: Your sales pipeline starts to dry up, and you suffer from the feast-or-famine sales roller coaster.

3. **Thank your team** whether in-house, outsourced, full-time, or virtual.

Ramifications if not done daily: Your team loses their motivation, momentum, and mojo. Once that's gone, they're halfway out the door.

4. **Offer value** in terms of content, your blog, a video, a resource, a referral, a favor, a gift.

Ramifications if not done daily: You become just more marketing noise, and clients and prospects tune you out and see you as a peddler, not a partner.

5. **Invite engagement** online, offline, in person, by phone or Zoom; ask and answer questions, solicit feedback, invite comments, send a survey.

Ramifications if not done daily: Your business becomes isolated as you talk AT your prospects and clients rather than talk WITH them.

6. **Recharge your batteries** because just like the airlines say, you need to "secure your own mask before assisting others."

Ramifications if not done daily: Entrepreneurial burnout, stress, drinking, drugs, and divorce. Don't laugh. You could be next.

7. **Be gracious and grateful** by taking a moment to appreciate what you have, what you've built, and who you get to serve each day.

Ramifications if not done daily: Instead of becoming more and more fulfilling, your business success becomes a trap, an exhausting race, and a never-ending contest that is impossible to win. Stop, smell the coffee, and count your blessings.

77 ALL YOU DO IS TALK

No one will value your expertise higher than you do.

Can I get an amen?

The truth is:

People pay what YOU decide your expertise is worth.

Not a penny less.

And not a penny more.

For example, once you've finished all the uncovering and exploring and digging and probing of your prospect's problems, say:

> *The investment for the program that directly addresses everything we just talked about is only $32K. Most clients start seeing [personal, professional, financial] results even before our program is over. If that's not the case, then one of us is not doing our job.* ***And it's not usually me.***

Funny line, right?

Most prospects smile when you deliver that line, but it's both important and 100 percent true.

It reinforces the fact that in the coaching, consulting, training, and advisory business, at the end of the day, all we do is talk.

It's strategic talk. Tactical talk. Exactly-how-to talk.

You can share exactly what to do and how to do it, what to say and how to say it.

You can spell out every piece of advice and every recommendation in extreme and explicit detail.

But if the client doesn't pick up the tools, if they don't get into action, if they don't implement any of your brilliant advice, whose fault is that?

News flash: Clients must take action. They must implement. They must make it real because it's their actions that create results.

Which brings us to...

N

What's Next?

CONCLUSION

Readers must take action too!

What will you DO with all these sales ideas, frameworks, and tools?

Your first step in moving from **information** (this book) to **implementation** (your results) is to grab all the free training, templates, resources, and companion tools waiting for you at **www.doitmarketing.com/selling**

In addition to the 77 sales tools, strategies, frameworks, and principles you just read, consider this a **bonus list** of 101 sales tips, each delivered as a 3-word reminder of the ideas in this book.

1. Be more courageous.	**11.** Celebrate small wins.
2. Stop prospecting blind.	**12.** Eliminate wasted steps.
3. Tune your radar.	**13.** Aim higher sooner.
4. Listen more deeply.	**14.** Never stop learning.
5. Action creates traction.	**15.** Give, give, give.
6. Try new things.	**16.** Plant seeds relentlessly.
7. Hang in there.	**17.** Stop wasting time.
8. Get better daily.	**18.** Hound dogs bark.
9. Begin with enthusiasm.	**19.** Alpha dogs buy.
10. Finish with flair.	**20.** Value + Time = Trust.

21. Do your homework.
22. Bring home bacon.
23. Seek higher ground.
24. Stop the crazy.
25. Start the money.
26. Give awesome gifts.
27. Keep it real.
28. Start fresh today.
29. Be the hero.
30. Write that letter.
31. Prove your case.
32. Trust the process.
33. Seize the day.
34. Solve prospect problems.
35. Make others shine.
36. Ask better questions.
37. Think WAY bigger.
38. Focus your energies.
39. Now beats later.
40. Let's play nice.
41. Zig, don't zag.
42. Never sell alone.
43. Stay the course.
44. Don't get distracted.
45. Always ask, "Why?"
46. Amp it up!
47. "How" doesn't matter.
48. Invite and engage.
49. You're already there.
50. Enjoy the ride.

51. Fascinate to dominate.
52. Write it down.
53. Keep on truckin'!
54. Love your clients.
55. Ask for help.
56. Never give up.
57. Make prospects friends.
58. Sharpen your edge.
59. Bang it out.
60. Serve to sell.
61. Speak your mind.
62. Expand your circles.
63. Use their numbers.
64. Consider crazy ideas.
65. Not so fast.
66. Go for no.
67. Blow 'em away.
68. Make miracles happen.
69. Stretch your possibilities.
70. Kill your ego.
71. It's about them.
72. Speak their language.
73. Earn their respect.
74. Don't shy away.
75. Give more generously.
76. Don't be scared.
77. Review your plan.
78. Freshen it up.
79. Ask dumb questions.

80. Anticipate common roadblocks.
81. Question their answers.
82. Pictures beat words.
83. Thank your heroes.
84. Respond, don't react.
85. Invest in yourself.
86. Seek the truth.
87. Avoid the obvious.
88. Birds gotta fly.
89. Fish gotta swim.
90. Relationships are perishable.
91. Make that call.
92. Track your progress.
93. Decisions drive momentum.
94. Take notes everywhere.
95. Look further ahead.
96. Stop playing small.
97. Sell the dream.
98. Deliver the goods.
99. Never shortchange yourself.
100. You're so ready.
101. DO IT. Now!

CONTINUE THE JOURNEY

Thank you for reading all the way to the end.

Of course, every ending is simply the beginning of something new. It's no different with this book.

To extend your learning, doing, and results, here are some resources, tools, and experiences to help YOU land better clients, bigger deals, and higher fees.

THE DO IT! MBA MENTORING EXPERIENCE

Intensive and personalized sales acceleration mentoring for consultants, coaches, speakers, and professional service providers who want to position themselves as thought leaders and win more clients, more easily, and more often.

Details at **www.doitmba.com.**

THE SELLING SHOW PODCAST

The Selling Show is an interview-based podcast ranked as a top-50 business podcast on Apple Podcasts focusing on the topic of selling professional services and geared to a core audience of B2B consultants, executive coaches, and thought-leading experts who want instant-action strategies, advice, and insights to grow their business.

Tune in and subscribe at **www.TheSellingShow.com**.

FREE SALES TRAINING AND MASTERCLASSES

Visit **www.doitmarketing.com/webinar** to get our latest on-demand sales training for consultants and business coaches ready to build, grow, and scale their expertise-based business.

We also run live master classes, sales labs, and 2-day virtual and in-person events throughout the year. Visit **www.doitmarketing.com/selling** to get the latest event schedule and all the companion resources for this book.

FREE BUSINESS ACCELERATOR CALL

We like talking with smart, ambitious experts who want to sell more, earn more, and become authorities in their fields. We'll take a 15-minute cruise through your positioning, packaging, marketing, prospecting, and pricing to help you see exactly what's working, what's not, and how to fix it. Sessions always fill quickly every month.

Visit **www.doitmarketing.com/call.**

FREE DO IT! MARKETING® MANIFESTO

Bad news: Marketing for the sake of marketing is broken. Kaput. Finished. Smart marketing is all about helping you generate more leads, better prospects, and bigger sales. Good news: that also happens to be the purpose of this powerful, action-packed manifesto you're about to read.

Visit **www.doitmarketing.com/manifesto.**

BECOME DO IT! MARKETING® CERTIFIED

If you're a small business coach, sales trainer, marketing consultant, or you run a digital marketing agency, and you want to **elevate your expertise** and add an **instant profit center** to your existing business using the complete array of Do It! Marketing and Do It! Selling tools, we should talk.

Several times a year, David personally trains a hand-selected cohort of smart experts to use our proprietary methodology, training, and tools as a seamless add-on to their existing consulting, coaching, speaking, training, or agency business.

For more information on the **Do It! Marketing Certified** application process, schedule, details, and investment, simply drop an email to **info@doitmarketing.com** with the subject line **"Do It! Marketing Certified Inquiry."**

LET'S STAY CONNECTED

in www.linkedin.com/in/davidjnewman

🐦 www.twitter.com/dnewman

▶ www.youtube.com/@dnewman

f www.facebook.com/groups/ThoughtLeadershipMarketing

📷 www.instagram.com/realdavidnewman

Email: david@doitmarketing.com

ACKNOWLEDGMENTS

First acknowledgment goes to **YOU.** You've read the book, and you're now about to embark on doing the work. I admire you and salute you. It's time to #DOIT!

For the record, I would **love, love, love** to hear from you, and I answer every reader email, so please don't hesitate to drop me a line. Heck, put this book down right now and email me at **david@ doitmarketing.com** to let me know you finished the book!

To all our **amazing clients** in the Do It! MBA mentorship, you're an ongoing inspiration for your effort, energy, tenacity, and smarts. The more you DO, the more results you get, and I speak for our whole team when I say how incredibly proud I am of the constant stream of breakthroughs, wins, and successes you are experiencing in your business. Yes, we're working alongside you with the support, mentorship, and guidance you want, but it is YOU who are doing the work and creating those game-changing 6- and 7-figure results. Let's keep going!

Finally, to the hardest-working crew in show business, a huge THANK YOU to our entire **Do It! Marketing team,** including Theresa, Allison, Ray, Katie, Amanda, Rina, Laura, Morgan, Rachel, Sam, and Charlie. I could not do this without your help, smarts, resourcefulness, kindness, patience, and professionalism. You serve our clients to the moon and back. And they get results commensurate with your enormous wisdom, skill, and dedication. Thank you for being YOU.

—David

P.S. Where are my **amazing family, friends, mentors, kids, and puppies** you ask? They were lavished with praise in the acknowledgments of both *Do It! Marketing* and *Do It! Speaking*. Please refer to those two books on your bookshelf if you're curious how blessed I am in my personal life. Because it's a LOT.

ABOUT THE AUTHOR

DAVID NEWMAN, CSP, is a professional services sales expert who works with leading consultants, coaches, and speakers who want to land better clients, bigger deals, and higher fees.

David is the author of the #1 business bestseller, *Do It! Marketing*, and he's the creator of the Do It! MBA mentorship (**www.doitmba.com**). David is the host of the highly rated podcast *The Selling Show*, with over 300 episodes.

David has been working at the intersection of marketing, sales, and professional services since 1992. His clients and audiences include Accenture, KPMG, Oracle, IBM, Microsoft, PWC, and 44 of the Fortune 500.

As a revenue growth mentor, David and his team have worked with over 1,800 successful consultants and business coaches.

David has been featured and quoted in the *New York Times*, *Investor's Business Daily*, *Forbes*, MSN, StartupNation, FastCompany.com, *Sales & Marketing Management*, *Selling Power*, Thrive Global, CNBC, and *Entrepreneur* magazine.

David is married to the #1 most amazing woman on the planet, launched two great kids into the world disguised as small adults, and has the world's sweetest English Cream Retriever named Gracie.

Free sales resources, templates, training, and tools are waiting for you online at **www.doitmarketing.com/selling**.